CRIME AND DETECTION

RACE AND CRIME

CRIME AND DETECTION

- Capital Punishment
- Criminal Terminology
- Cyber Crime
- Daily Prison Life
- Domestic Crime
- Famous Trials
- Forensic Science
- Global Terrorism
- Government Intelligence Agencies
- Hate Crimes
- The History of Punishment
- The History of Torture
- Infamous Prisons
- Organized Crime
- Protecting Yourself Against Criminals
- Race and Crime
- Serial Murders
- Unsolved Crimes
- The U.S. Justice System
- The War on Drugs

CRIME AND DETECTION

RACE AND CRIME

John Wright

Foreword by Manny Gomez, Esq.

MASON CREST

Mason Crest
450 Parkway Drive, Suite D
Broomall, PA 19008
www.masoncrest.com

Copyright © 2017 by Mason Crest, an imprint of National Highlights, Inc. All rights reserved. No part of this publication may be reproduced or transmitted in any form or by any means, electronic or mechanical, including photocopying, recording, taping, or any information storage and retrieval system, without permission in writing from the publisher.

Printed and bound in the United States of America

First printing
9 8 7 6 5 4 3 2 1

Series ISBN: 978-1-4222-3469-3
Hardcover ISBN: 978-1-4222-3485-3
ebook ISBN: 978-1-4222-8412-4

Library of Congress Cataloging-in-Publication Data on file with the Library of Congress

Developed and Produced by Print Matters Productions, Inc. (www.printmattersinc.com)

Developmental Editor: Amy Hackney Blackwell
Cover and Interior Design: Tom Carling, Carling Design Inc.

Note on Statistics: While every effort has been made to provide the most up-to-date government statistics, the Department of Justice and other agencies compile new data at varying intervals, sometimes as much as ten years. Agency publications are often based on data compiled from a period ending a year or two before the publication date.

CONTENTS

Foreword by Manny Gomez, Esq. 6
The Concept of Race 9
Racial Crimes in the United States 25
Dr. Martin Luther King, Jr. 45
Apartheid 57
Race Crimes in Other Nations 73

    Series Glossary 86

    Chronology 91

    Further Information 93

    Index 95

    Picture Credits 96

KEY ICONS TO LOOK FOR:

Text-Dependent Questions: These questions send the reader back to the text for more careful attention to the evidence presented there.

Words to Understand: These words with their easy-to-understand definitions will increase the reader's understanding of the text while building vocabulary skills.

Series Glossary of Key Terms: This back-of-the-book glossary contains terminology used throughout this series. Words found here increase the reader's ability to read and comprehend higher-level books and articles in this field.

Research Projects: Readers are pointed toward areas of further inquiry connected to each chapter. Suggestions are provided for projects that encourage deeper research and analysis.

Sidebars: This boxed material within the main text allows readers to build knowledge, gain insights, explore possibilities, and broaden their perspectives by weaving together additional information to provide realistic and holistic perspectives.

FOREWORD

Experience Counts

Detecting crime and catching lawbreakers is a very human endeavor. Even the best technology has to be guided by human intelligence to be used effectively. If there's one truth from my thirty years in law enforcement and security, it's trust your gut.

When I started on the police force, I learned from older officers and from experience what things to look for, what traits, characteristics, or indicators lead to somebody who is about to commit a crime or in the process of committing one. You learn from experience. The older generation of law enforcement teaches the younger generation, and then, if you're good, you pick up your own little nuances as to what bad guys are doing.

In my early work, I specialized in human intelligence, getting informants to tell me what was happening on the street. Most of the time it was people I arrested that I then "flipped" to inform me where the narcotics were being stored, how they were being delivered, how they were being sold, the patterns, and other crucial details.

A good investigator has to be organized since evidence must be presented in a legally correct way to hold up in court. Evidence from a crime scene has to have a perfect chain of custody. Any mishandling turns the evidence to fruits of a poisonous tree.

At my company, MG Security Services, which provides private security to corporate and individual clients in the New York area, we are always trying to learn and to pass on that learning to our security officers in the field.

Certainly, the field of detection has evolved dramatically in the last 100 years. Recording devices have been around for a long time; it's just that now they've gotten really good. Today, a pen can be a video recording device; whereas in the old days it would have been a large box with two wheels. The equipment was awkward and not too subtle: it would be eighty degrees out, you'd be sweating in a raincoat, and the box would start clicking.

The forensic part of detection is very high-tech these days, especially with DNA coming into play in the last couple of decades. A hundred years ago, fingerprinting revolutionized detective work; the next breakthrough is facial recognition. We have recently discovered that the arrangement of facial features (measured as nodes) is unique to each individual. No two people on the planet have the exact same configuration of nodes. Just as it took decades to build out the database of known fingerprints, facial recognition is a work in progress. We will see increasing collection of facial data when people obtain official identification. There are privacy concerns, but we're working them out. Facial recognition will be a centerpiece of future detection and prevention efforts.

Technology offers law enforcement important tools that we're learning to apply strategically. Algorithms already exist that allow retailers to signal authorities when someone makes a suspicious purchase—known bomb-making ingredients, for example. Cities are loaded with sensors to detect the slightest trace of nuclear, biological, or chemical materials that pose a threat to the public. And equipment nested on streetlights in New York City can triangulate the exact block where a gun was fired.

Now none of this does anything constructive without well-trained professionals ready and able to put the information to use. The tools evolve, but what doesn't evolve is human intelligence.

Law enforcement as a community is way ahead in fighting street and violent crime than the newer challenges of cybercrime and terrorism. Technology helps, but it all goes back to human intelligence. There is no substitute for the cop on the street, knowing what is going on in the neighborhood, knowing who the players are. When the cop has quality informants inside gangs, he or she knows when there's going to be a hit, a drug drop, or an illicit transaction. The human intelligence comes first; then you can introduce the technology, such as hidden cameras or other surveillance.

The twin challenges for domestic law enforcement are gangs and guns. Gangs are a big problem in this country. That's a cultural and social phenomenon that law enforcement has not yet found an effective way to counteract. We need to study that more diligently. If we're successful in getting rid of the gangs, or at least diluting them, we will have come a long way in fighting violent crime. But guns are the main issue. You look at England, a first-world country of highly educated people that strictly regulates guns, and the murder rate is minimal.

When it comes to cybercrime, we're woefully behind. That's simply because we hire people for the long term, and their skills get old. You have a twenty-five-year-old who's white-hot now, but guess what? In five years that skill set is lost. Hackers, on the other hand, are young people who tend to evolve fast. They learn so much more than their older law-enforcement counterparts and are able to penetrate systems too easily. The Internet was not built with the security of private users in mind. It is like a house with no door locks, and now we're trying to figure ways to secure the house. It was done kind of backward. Nobody really thought that it was going to be this wide-open door to criminal activity.

We need to change the equation for cybercriminals. Right now the chances are they won't get caught; cybercrime offers criminals huge benefit at very little cost. Law enforcement needs to recruit young people who can match skills with the criminals. We also need to work closely with foreign governments and agencies to better identify, deter, and apprehend cybercriminals. We need to make examples of them.

Improving our cybercrime prevention means a lot more talent, a lot more resources, a lot more hands-on collaboration with countries on the outskirts—Russia, China, even Israel. These are the countries that are constantly trying to penetrate our cyberspace. And even if we are able to identify the person overseas, we still need the cooperation of the overseas government and law enforcement to help us find and apprehend the person. Electrical grids are extremely vulnerable to cyber attacks. Utilities built long before the Internet need engineering retrofits to make them better able to withstand attacks.

As with cybercrime, efforts against terrorism must be coordinated to be effective. Communication is crucial among all levels of law enforcement, from local law enforcement and national agencies sharing information—in both directions—to a similar international flow of information among different countries' governments and national bureaus.

In the U.S., since 9/11, the FBI and local law enforcement now share a lot more information with each other locally and nationally. Internationally, as well, we are sharing more information with Interpol and other intelligence and law enforcement agencies throughout the world to be able to better detect, identify, and prevent criminal activity.

When it comes to terrorism, we also need to ramp up our public relations. Preventing terror attacks takes more than a military response. We need to address this culture of death with our own Internet media campaign and 800 numbers to make it easy for people to reach out to law enforcement and help build the critical human infrastructure. Without people, there are no leads—people on the inside of a criminal enterprise are essential to directing law enforcement resources effectively, telling you when to listen, where to watch, and which accounts to check.

In New York City, the populace is well aware of the "see something, say something" campaign. Still, we need to do more. More people need to speak up. Again, it comes down to trusting your instincts. If someone seems a little off to you, find a law enforcement representative and share your perception. Listen to your gut. Your gut will always tell you: there's something hinky going on here. Human beings have a sixth sense that goes back to our caveman days when animals used to hunt us. So take action, talk to law enforcement when something about a person makes you uneasy or you feel something around you isn't right.

We have to be prepared not just on the prevention side but in terms of responses. Almost every workplace conducts a fire drill at least once a year. We need to do the same with active-shooter drills. Property managers today may even have their own highly trained active-shooter teams, ready to be on site within minutes of any attack.

We will never stop crime, but we can contain the harm it causes. The coordinated efforts of law enforcement, an alert and well-trained citizenry, and the smart use of DNA, facial profiles, and fingerprinting will go a long way toward reducing the number and severity of terror events.

Be it the prevention of street crime or cybercrime, gang violence or terrorism, sharing information is essential. Only then can we put our technology to good use. People are key to detection and prevention. Without the human element, I like to say a camera's going to take a pretty picture of somebody committing a crime.

Law enforcement must strive to attract qualified people with the right instincts, team-sensibility, and work ethic. At the end of the day, there's no hunting like the hunting of man. It's a thrill; it's a rush; and that to me is law enforcement in its purest form.

MANNY GOMEZ, Esq.

President of MG Security Services,

Chairman of the National Law Enforcement Association,

former FBI Special Agent,

U.S. Marine, and NYPD Sergeant

Foreword

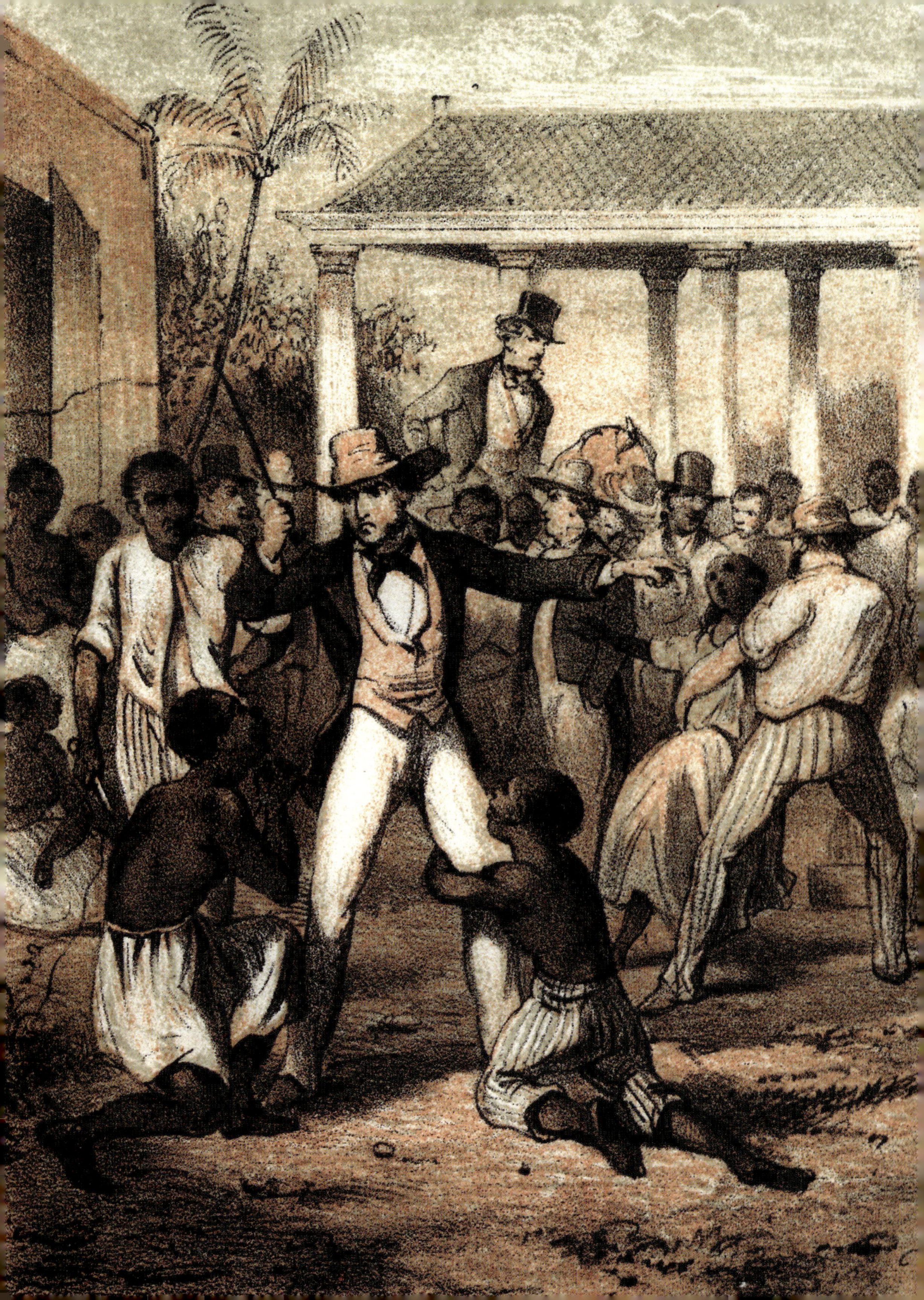

CHAPTER 1

THE CONCEPT OF RACE

Words to Understand

Abolitionists: people who are opposed to slavery

Anthropologists: scientists who study humans and their cultures

Ethnic cleansing: brutal program to kill or remove people of a certain ethnic background

Guest workers: foreigners who are working in another country; the term is especially used in Germany, France, and other European nations

Holocaust: the Nazis' mass killing of Jews during World War II

Immigrants: people from other nations who come and settle in a new country

Nationalism: love of and pride in one's country

Patriotism: special love and devotion for one's country

Political asylum: act of letting a foreigner settle in your country to escape danger in another country, usually his or her native land

Racism: a belief that race is the primary determinant of human traits and capacities and that racial differences produce an inherent superiority of a particular race

Slavery was one of the worst crimes in history, and it still exists in some parts of the world. The most organized traffic in human beings was initially carried out by Europeans, who enslaved Africans to work in the New World.

CRIMES ARE NOT COMMITTED BECAUSE DIFFERENT RACES EXIST. THEY HAPPEN BECAUSE SOME PEOPLE BELIEVE THE DEEP-ROOTED, BUT WRONG, IDEAS THAT ALL MEMBERS OF A RACE HAVE THE SAME BAD CHARACTERISTICS, LIKE BEING LAZY, DEVIOUS, OR SLOW-WITTED, AND THAT SOME RACES ARE MORE INTELLIGENT AND BETTER THAN OTHERS. MANY PEOPLE BELIEVE THAT THE "BEST" RACE IS THEIR OWN.

How Races Are Classified

What is a race? We usually think about members of a race as having the same skin color, facial features, type of hair, and other similar looks. People have often used biology to divide the races, since each type has inherited different genes. Using this idea, **anthropologists** in the 19th century decided that only three races exist: Caucasoid (white), Mongoloid (yellow or red), and Negroid (black).

Today, many scientists consider racial groups less important than ethnic groups, whose members have many different things in common, like culture, language, religion, and social institutions. Americans also use "ethnic" to mean nonwhite minorities, as in "ethnic food" and "ethnic music." Some crimes against ethnic groups are also called race crimes, because the word "race" is used in a general way.

One problem is that few people know exactly what race is. The U.S. Census Bureau divides race into five main classifications: white (including Arabs and North Africans), black or African American, Native American (including South and Central America) and Alaska natives, Asian, and native Hawaiian and other Pacific Islanders. These categories were introduced in 1997. The 2010 census also asked about ethnicity, whether a person was of Hispanic or Latino origin. For the 2020 census, the bureau is considering dropping the categories of race and origin, and allowing people to choose from various categories that better describe them. This is because people are confused about the meaning of race, and many believe that "Hispanic" is a racial description.

Throughout history, people have put insulting labels on other races and groups that looked and acted differently from theirs. Even the supposedly enlightened thinkers did this. The Greek philosopher Aristotle (384–322 B.C.) said Asians were lazy. The Swedish physician Carolus Linnaeus (1707–1778) thought whites were gentle, blacks were stubborn, and Asians were greedy. Pierre

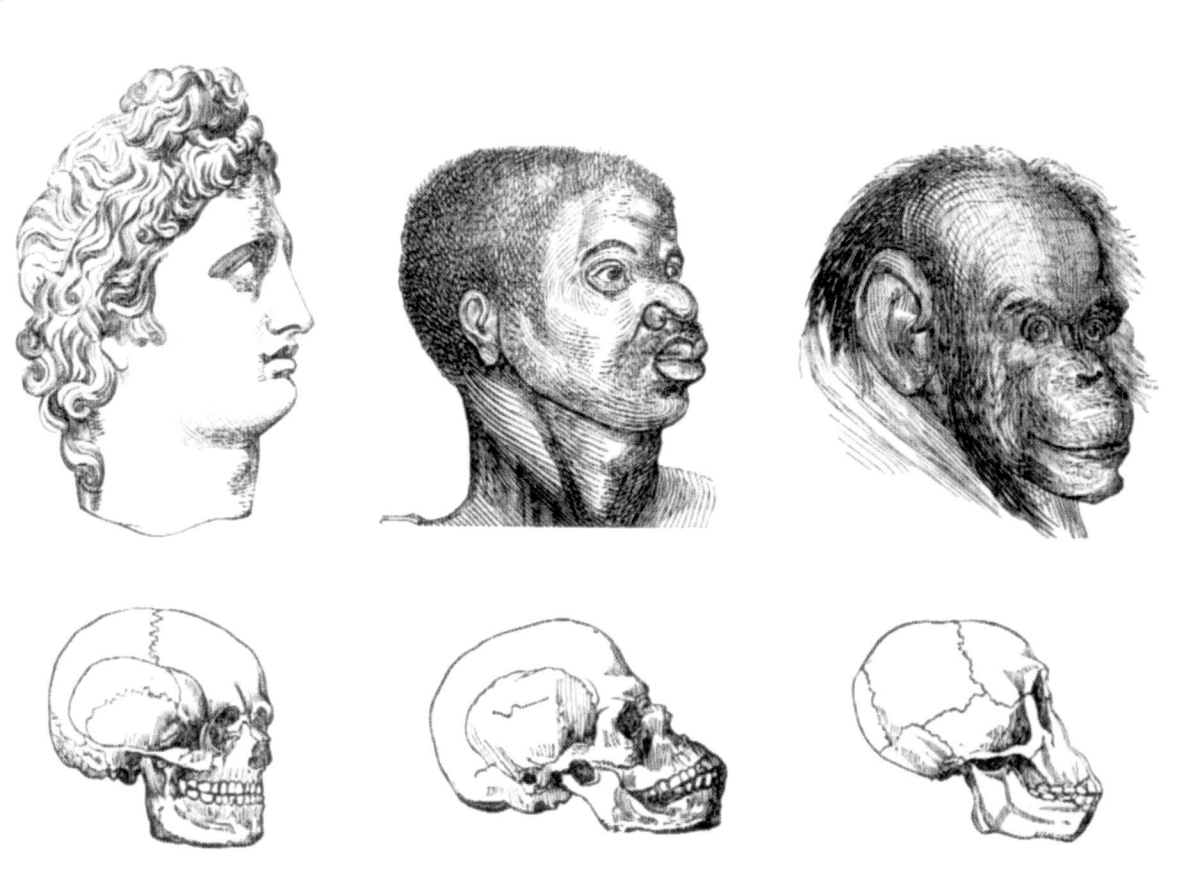

The Victorians believed the white race was more advanced than others. This 1854 diagram supposedly showed how skull shapes had evolved to the ideal European one (copied from a Greek sculpture). The implication was that other races were more primitive and less advanced.

Paul Broca (1824–1880), the Frenchman who began the first Society of Anthropology, said white people were the furthest from the apes and superior to all other races. And the English writer Rudyard Kipling (1865–1936) wrote a poem called "The White Man's Burden" about having to civilize colonial people who were "half-devil and half-child."

From the beginning of history, this feeling of superiority over other types of people has encouraged more powerful groups to conquer less-advantaged ones. Strangers were almost always feared and disliked. The word "barbarian" is a word that is now used to mean a savage, but it was an ancient Greek word for a foreigner. The Romans ruled tribes in Britain, and nearly 2,000 years later, the British ruled tribes in Africa and were one of the European nations that developed the slave trade there.

The *Amistad* Rebellion

The mutiny of slaves in 1839 on the slave ship *La Amistad* (Friendship) was a major event that changed the way the U.S. legal system looked at slavery. Their action also became a symbol for slaves' long struggle for freedom. The story began when Portuguese slave hunters captured many people in the African country of Sierra Leone and shipped them to Havana, Cuba. Spanish planters bought 53 (including four children) and put them on the Cuban schooner *La Amistad* bound for a Caribbean plantation. On the third night out—July 1, 1839—a slave named Cinque led the other slaves in a revolt to take over the ship, killing the captain and cook. They ordered the remaining crew to sail back to Africa toward the rising sun, but each night the crew secretly turned the ship back west. After two months of this zigzag movement, the currents and winds took *La Amistad* off Long Island, New York, where a U.S. revenue ship seized it. The slaves were imprisoned in New Haven, Connecticut, as property.

President Martin Van Buren wanted to send the Africans back to Cuba, but **abolitionists** raised money to defend the prisoners. The case went to the U.S. Supreme Court in January 1841, and former president John Quincy Adams helped attorney Roger Sherman Baldwin defend the slaves, who spoke no English. Adams and Baldwin said that international law meant that the Africans had been bought illegally. The Supreme Court justices agreed, and the *Amistad* mutineers were freed and allowed to sail back to their homeland. Steven Spielberg's 1997 movie, *Amistad*, made the story known around the world.

Slavery and Nationhood

Forcing a race of people into slavery to serve another race is an extreme example of **racism**. For instance, white Europeans, including those who settled the United States, made captives of black Africans and even pretended it was for the slaves' own good. Some blacks in Africa helped capture slaves for Western nations, and a few tribes owned slaves from other groups. More than 1,000 blacks in the United States even owned black slaves themselves. The Confederate president, Jefferson Davis, said slaves had been "elevated" from brutal savages into docile, intelligent, and civilized agricultural laborers, and supplied not only with bodily comforts, but also with careful religious instruction under the supervision of a superior "race." Other races around the world also owned slaves. The Arabs, for instance, were traditional slave owners.

A painting of Cinque, the leader of the *Amistad* slave rebellion.

PLAN OF LOWER DECK WITH THE STOWAGE OF 292 SLAVES
130 OF THESE BEING STOWED UNDER THE SHELVES AS SHEWN IN FIGURE B & FIGURE 5.

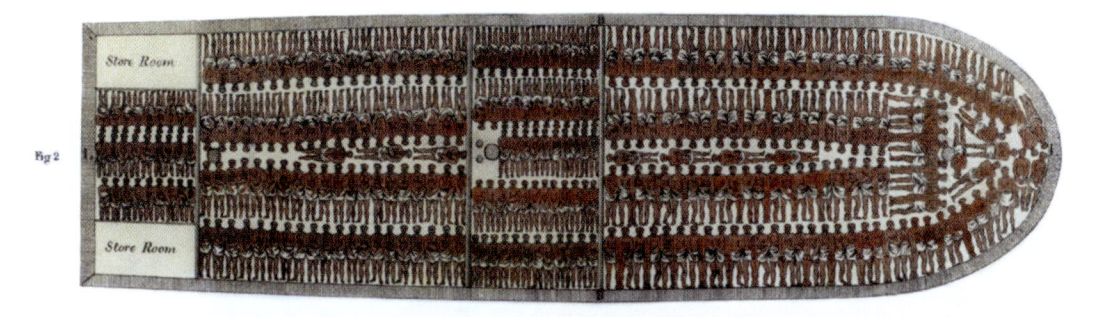

Fig 2

PLAN SHEWING THE STOWAGE OF 130 ADDITIONAL SLAVES ROUND THE WINGS OR SIDES OF THE LOWER DECK BY MEANS OF PLATFORMS OR SHELVES (IN THE MANNER OF GALLERIES IN A CHURCH) THE SLAVES STOWED ON THE SHELVES AND BELOW THEM HAVE ONLY A HEIGHT OF 2 FEET 7 INCHES BETWEEN THE BEAMS: AND FAR LESS UNDER THE BEAMS. See Fig 1.

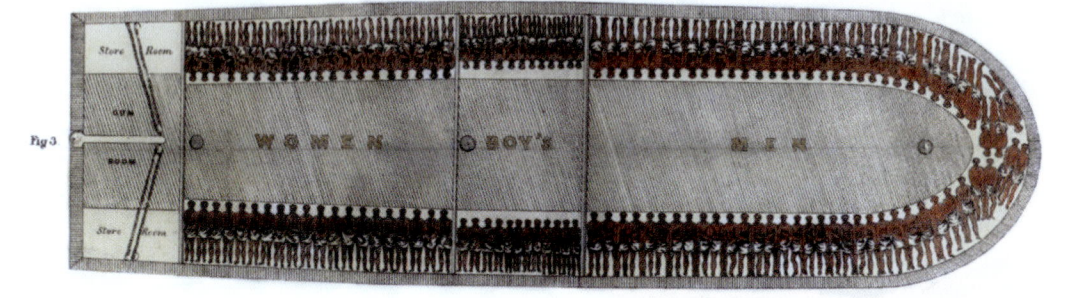

Fig 3

One of the horrors facing African slaves bound for America was the long sea voyage. They were packed into small spaces below deck and usually chained. They often became weak and ill, which caused many deaths. This 1790 poster from a British group opposed to the slave trade shows the inhumane crowding of a standard slave ship.

A nation is not a race. For instance, there is no French race, because a French person is anybody who lives in France. The United States is a very good example of a nation created for all types of people, and Americans are proud to be called the "melting pot" of different races and ethnic groups.

A strong feeling of **nationalism** and **patriotism** can have good or bad consequences. Many wars have begun because two nations wanted the same land. This caused the tragic conflict between the Palestinians, who want to be recognized as a nation, and the Israelis. However, love for your own country can also bring together the various races and ethnic groups. A good example is Canada, whose citizens are the descendants of British, French, and Inuit people, yet they all live comfortably together in one country as a single nation.

Holocaust Statistics

The Nazis' grievous crime of killing Jews during World War II is called the **Holocaust**, because a holocaust is a great destruction or slaughter of people. It is difficult to estimate the exact number of Jews killed during "the final solution," which was the Nazi name for this program of mass murder. The total deaths were about six million. The 10 countries that lost the largest number of their Jewish populations were (with estimated deaths):

1. Poland (3,000,000)
2. Soviet Union (1,100,000)
3. Hungary (450,000–596,000)
4. Germany (141,500–200,000)
5. Romania (287,000)
6. Lithuania (143,000)
7. Netherlands (100,000)
8. Latvia (71,500–80,000)
9. France (77,320)
10. Bohemia/Moravia (71,150)

The Concept of Race

Nazi Germany and Ethnic Cleansing

The most tragic example of mixing nationalism with racism in the 20th century is the Nazi era in Germany. Adolf Hitler admired the Aryan people who had moved from Eastern Europe into Germany long ago. He considered them to be a superior race of blue-eyed, blond-haired people, and felt that they should be kept pure. He also convinced the Germans that they could be (and, indeed, deserved to be) the masters of Europe, which led to the Germans' attempt to dominate Europe with military force, thus starting World War II.

There was an even worse side to Hitler's racism. He believed the Jews were an inferior race who had caused financial ruin and other problems in Germany. This idea led to one of the greatest race crimes in history when the Nazi Party killed Jews throughout Germany and in every country they conquered. The total deaths in Nazi gas chambers numbered about six million. (The Nazis also murdered other people they labeled as "defective," including Gypsies, people with physical disabilities, and homosexuals.)

This horrible crime shocked the world so badly that most people thought mass racial and ethnic killings would never occur again. Sadly, it happened in the 1990s in Yugoslavia, a country where the Nazis had killed more than 63,000 Jews some 50 years earlier. Four different areas of Yugoslavia declared their independence, and fighting began among ethnic groups. It was especially bad in Bosnia, where the Serbs engaged in **ethnic cleansing** to remove or kill the local Muslim population. Then, in 1999, American-led NATO forces had to bomb Yugoslavian forces that were driving out ethnic Albanians from the Kosovo region.

Seeking Asylum and Worldwide Immigration

Worldwide immigration has presented a new problem in the 21st century. Since World War II, many people from poor and less advantaged nations have sought a better life in both North America and Europe. Some ask for **political asylum**, which means they are seeking protection from their own governments. At first, the richer countries encouraged them. Migrant workers from Mexico provided cheap labor for U.S. farms, and southern Europeans were needed

Residents of Cernica, Kosovo, pass in front of a window broken by rocks thrown during ethnic clashes. Hatred between the Serbs and Albanians was only one of the conflicts occurring between groups in the Balkan area.

The Concept of Race   17

as **guest workers** in Germany, France, and other nations that had lost many able-bodied workers in the war. Even today, they are needed because of low birth rates in northern Europe.

As the gap between rich and poor countries has grown, so have illegal **immigrants**. People who once welcomed immigrants are now worried that these poorer people will lower their nation's standard of living. In 2000, Austria surprised the world by electing members of the anti-immigrant Austrian Freedom Party to its government. When the United States was attacked on September 11, 2001, by Islamic terrorists, Western countries began to worry about their increasing foreign populations, wondering if they were unwittingly harboring terrorists posing as legal immigrants. By the 2010s, some residents of European nations were feeling overwhelmed by the increasing numbers of refugees and illegal immigrants trying to enter their borders. Hundreds of would-be immigrants died in the Mediterranean when overloaded ships sank or in the backs of trucks. Thousands more entered Europe and tried to establish themselves in their new homes. This has caused increasing friction between the immigrants and the nations they hope will receive them.

The U.S. government, while tightening its borders against terrorists, is working hard to ease racial and ethnic tensions. President George W. Bush moved quickly after September 11, 2001, to protect American Muslims from prejudice and hate crimes, and the Department of Justice held meetings in several cities to stop ethnic violence. Additional help came from the many American organizations that constantly work to eliminate the types of crimes mentioned in the next chapter of this book. The work has continued through the 2010s as racial and ethnically based crimes continue to occur in the United States and other countries.

In 2015, many Western countries saw an overwhelming increase in refugees coming to their countries. Many refugees traveled the Mediterranean in small boats, such as this, to escape their country in hope of escaping poverty and violence at home.

The Concept of Race

The Tutsi and the Hutu

The Tutsi and Hutu are the two largest ethnic groups in the central African countries of Rwanda and Burundi. They have fought one another for over 500 years, since the Tutsi came into the area from Ethiopia in the 15th century. The Tutsis are a tall people who have mostly tended cattle, while the Hutu are traditionally farmers. An unsuccessful Hutu rebellion in Burundi in 1972 left 160,000 people dead, and a three-year ethnic conflict beginning in 1993 killed another 150,000 people.

One of the worst ethnic massacres in history occurred in 1994 in Rwanda, when more than 500,000 Tutsi people were killed by Hutu militias. This came after the Hutu president was killed that year in a suspicious plane crash. The mass killings forced two million Tutsis to become refugees in Zaire (now Congo), where many died of starvation and disease. In 1996, a moderate Hutu became Rwanda's president, and most refugees returned to their farms, but found many of them occupied by Hutus.

The Palestinian-Israeli Question

The conflict between Palestinians and Israelis can be traced back to 1947, when the United Nations voted to give about half of Palestine to Jewish settlers. This was to help them and give them a homeland after the horrors of the Holocaust.

In 1948, Israel declared its independence as a sovereign nation and Palestinians left the Jewish section as refugees. Arab countries attacked Israel unsuccessfully that year and again in 1967, when Israel won the Six Day War and gained the West Bank, Gaza, and Sinai.

The violence still continued in the 2010s, with both Palestinian suicide bombers and Israeli troops causing many civilian casualties. Both sides have demands that may be incompatible and which certainly make it difficult to reach a compromise. The Israelis want the Palestinians and other Arabs to recognize their right to exist as a nation and for the Palestinians to renounce terrorism. The Palestinians want their own nation-state, a joint rule in Jerusalem, the closing of Israeli settlements in Palestinian territory, and the right of Palestinian refugees to return to their original homes in Israel.

The UN General Assembly made Palestine a "non-member observer state" in 2012. By 2014, there was increasing worldwide support of recognition of the State of Palestine. Israel continued to object strenuously, supported by the United States and Canada. Violence continues in the region.

Demonstrators gather to support the passage of legislation that would give thousands of immigrants a legal status in the United States. Immigrant groups are often the target of racist attacks.

Text-Dependent Questions

1. What is race?
2. What is racism?
3. What is slavery?

Research Projects

1. What is the difference between race and ethnicity? Why should that matter?
2. What was the Holocaust? Why did it happen?
3. Why are thousands of people currently seeking asylum in other countries?

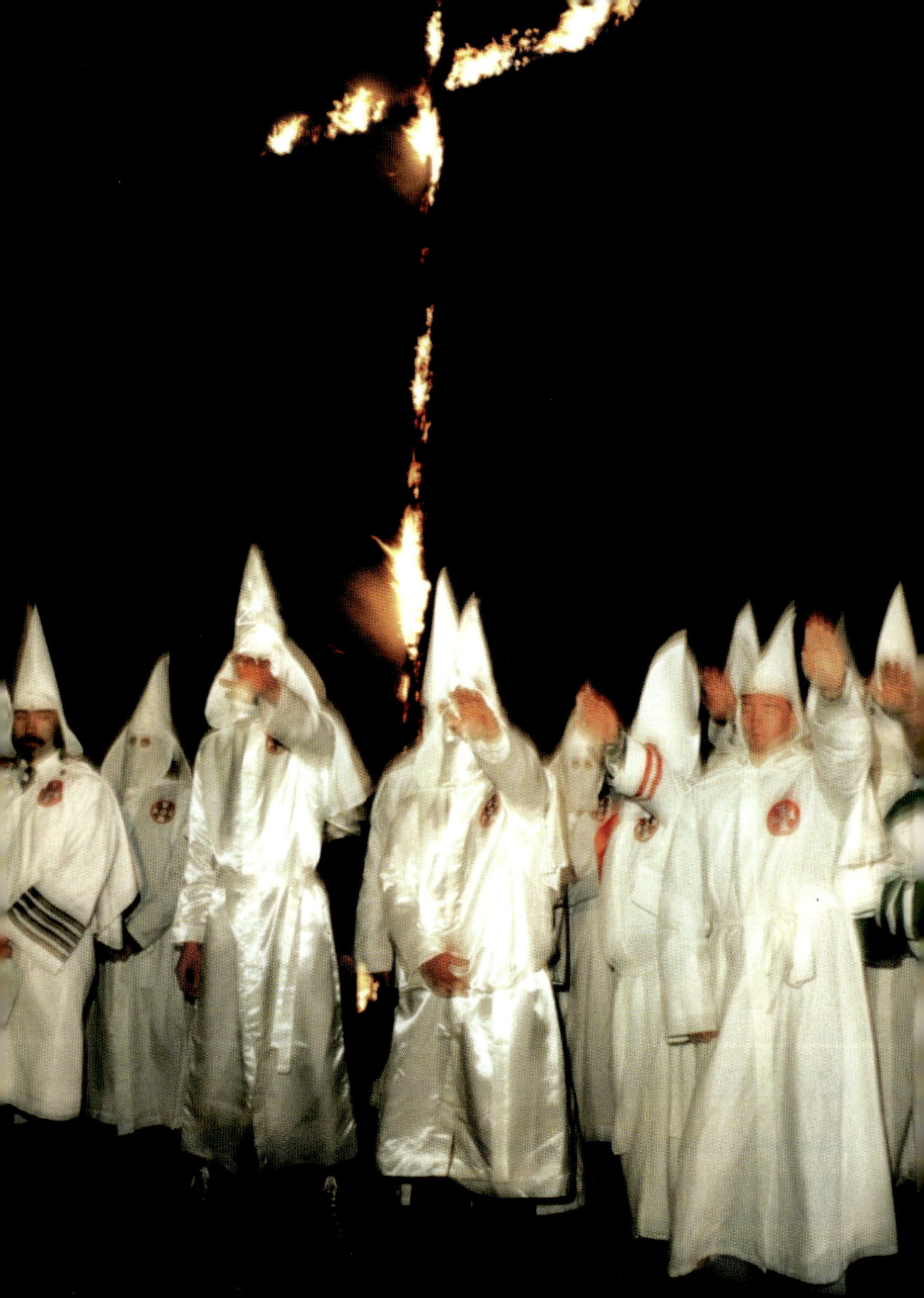

RACIAL CRIMES IN THE UNITED STATES

CHAPTER 2

Words to Understand

Acquit: to discharge completely from an accusation

Anti-Semitism: hostility toward or discrimination against Jews as a religious, ethnic, or racial group

Bigotry: acts or beliefs consistent with a person obstinately or intolerantly devoted to his or her own opinions and prejudices

Lynching: illegal killing of a person by a mob; this has usually referred to the hanging of a black person in the South

Sit-ins: tactics used by African Americans in restaurants that would not serve them; they would sit down at tables and refuse to move

The Ku Klux Klan promotes fear and hate by burning the cross and wearing white robes and masks. The Klan has been the largest organized racist organization in the nation, but its numbers fell in the late 20th century.

PRESIDENT JOHN F. KENNEDY CALLED THE UNITED STATES A "NATION OF IMMIGRANTS," BECAUSE OUR COUNTRY HAS TAKEN IN MORE DIFFERENT RACES AND ETHNIC GROUPS THAN ALMOST ANY OTHER IN THE WORLD'S HISTORY. ALMOST ALL OF US ARE DESCENDANTS OF IMMIGRANTS. THEY CAME IN SEARCH OF FREEDOM, DEMOCRACY, AND OPPORTUNITY, OR TO ESCAPE PREJUDICE AND VIOLENCE IN THEIR HOMELANDS. OTHERS CAME AS SLAVES AND HAD TO STRUGGLE FOR LIBERTY, EQUAL RIGHTS, AND RESPECT BEFORE SHARING IN THE AMERICAN DREAM. CREATING A NEW UNIFIED COUNTRY WAS NOT EASY FOR PEOPLE WHO HAD DIFFERENT CULTURES AND LANGUAGES. OLD FEARS AND PREJUDICES SOMETIMES LINGERED ON.

New American Settlers and the Native Americans

This was seen when the European explorers, colonists, and pioneers came in contact with Native Americans. Although fine examples of cooperation happened, both races mistrusted and feared the other. Each launched unprovoked attacks as the white settlers moved into Native American lands. Creek warriors killed 250 people at Fort Mims in Alabama on August 30, 1813. This was the worst Native American massacre of whites living east of the Mississippi River. However, the saddest result was how the Native Americans were treated as a conquered people and forced off their lands. The U.S. government even broke treaties with some Native American groups and ordered them to move west. In 1838, for example, the Cherokees were forced to move from Georgia to Oklahoma, and thousands died on this long journey that has been called the "Trail of Tears" because of the sorrow it caused.

Between 1860 and 1890, about 10 million immigrants entered the United States, finding new opportunities and a better life. They sometimes met with discrimination from established Americans, and even from members of other immigrant groups.

Several funds have been established to try and compensate Native Americans for this 19th-century injustice. The U.S. Department of the Interior manages millions of dollars in the Individual Indian Monies Trust to compensate tribes for lands taken. Funds and programs for Native Americans have also been put in place in several states, from Alaska to North Carolina. Many tribes are managing their lands successfully, with a National Tribal Environmental Council formed for all tribes.

Most of the native peoples, however, have moved off reservations and into mainstream America. By 1970, nearly three-quarters lived in cities. New casinos run by and for Native Americans are also generating income in the 21st century.

Although land was plentiful, the European settlers broke treaties with Native Americans and moved them onto reservations. Many groups still live there, such as this Navajo reservation.

The original Ku Klux Klan looked somewhat different just after the Civil War. The costumes had red braid holes bordered around the eyes, nose, and mouth. This was intended to scare African Americans and keep them "in their place."

The Oppression of Black Americans

The main race problem in U.S. history, of course, has been the discrimination and violence against African Americans and other people of color. Although the South was the greatest offender by continuing slavery, this system also existed in the North just before the Civil War. (Even General Ulysses S. Grant, who led the Union armies to victory, had slaves a mere six years before the war.) The worst race crime during the war occurred in New York City. Up to 50,000 people there rioted against the draft on July 13, 1863. The ensuing mob killed more than 100 blacks, blaming them for being the cause of the war. They also burned down a black church and orphanage before soldiers and police restored order. So African Americans were the butt of racial hatred in the North, too.

After the war, more crimes were committed against the freed slaves. The Ku Klux Klan (KKK) was formed in 1866 in Tennessee to frighten these new black citizens. The KKK members wore hoods and white sheets to play on their victims' belief in vengeful ghosts, and they burned crosses in front of their homes. This was a campaign to keep whites as the ruling race. This organization officially ended in 1869, but a new Klan was organized in 1915 and operated even in the North. Besides attacking blacks, it also declared itself against Roman Catholics, Jews, and foreigners. Ku Klux Klan membership was claimed to be nearly five million in the 1920s, but had dropped to about 13,000 in the 1980s. The KKK is still around, though; as of 2012 it boasted between 5,000 and 8,000 members.

Black Americans remained second-class citizens during the first half of the 20th century. The South had created a segregation system to keep the races apart. Black people had to sit at the backs of buses and in the balconies of movie theaters. They were not allowed in city parks and public swimming pools. Even public water fountains were labeled "white" and "colored." In the important area of education, two school systems were established using the idea of "separate but equal" that was approved by the U.S. Supreme Court (although the black schools were poorer). An unofficial type of segregation was practiced in many other parts of the nation that did not have written, formal segregation laws. African Americans found it hard to get good jobs.

An Olympic Protest

An Olympic medal is a joyous achievement, but two black American sprinters turned their victories into a bitter protest at the 1968 games in Mexico City. Tommie Smith won the gold medal in the 200-meter race and John Carlos took the bronze. Standing on the podium as "The Star-Spangled Banner" was played and the U.S. flag raised, both men bowed their heads and raised a black-gloved fist in the traditional black-power salute. Ordinary Americans were shocked, and the two athletes were immediately suspended from the national team and banned from the Olympic Village. They later received death threats.

Both were from San Jose State University in California. Smith set seven individual world track records and later played football for the Cincinnati Bengals. Carlos set the world record in the 100-yard dash and played football for the Philadelphia Eagles. They embarrassed their country before a worldwide audience, but have since helped develop future American athletes: Smith has been a track-and-field coach at Oberlin College in Ohio and Santa Monica College in California; Carlos has worked for the Olympics and is track-and-field coach for Palm Springs High School in California.

Racism in Times of War and Peace

All this institutional racism fortified the idea that black Americans were an inferior race. And it encouraged more race crimes. Mob killings were terrible acts that happened primarily from the 1880s to the 1940s. They shocked most Americans, and campaigns were instigated to stop **lynchings**, which were usually the illegal hanging of a black person by a group who decided the victim had broken a real law or a strong social taboo, like the "rule" against dating a white person. Some estimates say nearly 5,000 people were lynched, most of them African Americans.

Lynching was the most brutal form of racism in the South. Mobs illegally executed these victims, whom they accused of committing real or imaginary crimes or breaking social taboos.

RACE AND CRIME

Harry Truman was the first U.S. president in the 20th century to support civil rights for all Americans. Many of his ideas, such as ending segregation, were ahead of his time, but they became part of the civil rights movement.

Even during the two world wars, black citizens were not allowed to fight alongside whites, and the U.S. military formed separate units for African Americans. The racial group in the United States that suffered the most during World War II was the Japanese Americans. Along the Pacific coast, there were already anti-Asian feelings. The U.S. government worried that the Japanese Americans would act as spies or otherwise help Japan, our enemy at that time, to invade the Western states.

For this reason, the Army forced about 110,000 Japanese Americans on the West Coast to sell their homes and businesses and move inland to detention camps, called "relocation centers." They had to remain there throughout the war. Congress passed the Civil Rights Act of 1988, which apologized for interning them and provided $20,000 to every survivor. It said this was to discourage such an event from ever happening again and to uphold human rights.

The Civil Rights Movement

After the war, President Harry S. Truman became the first president since Lincoln to support strong civil-rights legislation. He ended segregation in the armed forces, opposed it in the government, and asked for a law that would make lynching a federal crime (but Congress refused to pass it). Many people credit Truman with creating the right national mood for the civil rights movement.

School segregation was finally declared illegal by the U.S. Supreme Court in 1954, after a school for white children in Topeka, Kansas, had refused to accept a black student. The government now gave African Americans full equal rights, but these were often ignored in the South. To make sure the laws were kept, Martin Luther King, Jr. and other blacks led the civil rights movement, which had many successes, especially from 1955 to 1965. One tactic they used was known as **sit-ins** and involved blacks sitting down at tables and taking up space in cafés and restaurants that refused to serve them. Protesters also used boycotts by refusing to shop at stores that did not hire African Americans.

All these events led to more race crimes by people opposing integration, the process of mixing the races in schools, restaurants, and other public places. Much of the violence was caused by groups of racists who traveled to civil rights events to stir up the local population. This happened in 1961, to oppose black and white people from the North who took "freedom rides" to the South in buses to break down the custom of blacks having to sit in the rear of a bus. Angry crowds sometimes attacked them, and a few buses were stoned and burned. The freedom riders won, however, when the U.S. Interstate Commerce Commission declared segregation illegal on buses that same year.

"Freedom riders," who tested segregation in the South, were met by angry crowds. This bus had a flat tire near Anniston, Alabama. A crowd gathered and one person tossed a fire bomb in the window, but nobody was injured.

State and city governments also broke the new federal law. When a black student was enrolled in the previously white University of Mississippi in 1962, the state's governor told whites to resist, and a racist riot on campus killed two people and injured 160 federal marshals. A year later, police in Birmingham, Alabama, used dogs and fire hoses against people who were peacefully demonstrating for integration.

Malcolm X and the Black Power Movement

Extremist black organizations were formed in response to the racism. The Black Panther Party was established in 1966 and supported violence to secure black rights. Malcolm X, an African American who helped develop the black power movement, became a spokesman for the Black Muslims and he, too, urged African Americans to use violence to defend themselves. He was an intelligent

Malcolm X (right), the Black Muslim leader, meets with Cassius Clay, the heavyweight boxing champion, in Harlem on March 1, 1964. Clay joined the Muslims that year and changed his name to Muhammad Ali.

man and a powerful speaker who influenced many blacks, but frightened whites with his hatred for them. The black power movement in the 1960s and 1970s seemed very threatening to many white Americans. In the last year of his life, however, Malcolm X began to seek a brotherhood between blacks and whites.

He was born as Malcolm Little in 1925 in Omaha, Nebraska, the son of a Baptist preacher, and raised in Lansing, Michigan, and then Boston before settling in New York. While doing a prison sentence for burglary from 1946–1952, he joined the Black Muslims and changed his name to Malcolm X (saying it replaced his "slave name"). When released, he became a leader of the Black Muslims, known formally as the Nation of Islam. Supporting the separation of an African-American nation, he called whites "devils" and told blacks to arm themselves for self-defense.

In 1963, he disagreed with the organization's leader, Elijah Muhammad. A year later, he made a pilgrimage to Mecca, the holy city of Muslims, and converted to the orthodox Islamic religion. Subsequently, he founded the Organization of Afro-American Unity, and he now supported social reform, looking forward to the races living and working together. In 1965, Malcolm X was shot and killed while addressing an audience in New York's Harlem district. Members of the Black Muslims were suspected of responsibility for the crime.

Resorting to Violence

This violence increased with the murders of civil rights activists, black and white. Medgar Evers, a black Mississippi official for the National Association for the Advancement of Colored People (NAACP), was shot and killed in front of his home by a racist in 1963. (It was 31 years before the murderer was convicted and sent to prison.) That same year, four black girls were killed when their Baptist church was bombed in Birmingham, Alabama. (An ex-KKK member was not convicted until 2001.) In 1964, three civil rights workers were murdered in Mississippi and seven white men were convicted. The next year, a white minister, James Reeb, was murdered while taking part in a march outside Selma, Alabama. Then, in 1968, the nation was shocked by the assassination of Martin Luther King, Jr.

George Wallace

Not many people have changed their racial views as much as the Alabama governor, George Wallace (1919–1998). In the 1960s, he was a symbol of white supremacy and vowed, "Segregation now. Segregation tomorrow. Segregation forever." In 1963, Wallace stood in a doorway at the University of Alabama to block the entrance of two black students who wanted to register, but he quickly stepped aside when the federal government took control of his state's National Guard. Wallace ran for president in 1968 as the American Independent Party candidate,

Racial Crimes in the United States 37

saying he was against integration and too much federal control. He received a surprising 13.5 percent of the popular vote. Reelected governor in 1971, he ran for the Democratic party's presidential nomination in 1972, but was shot in a crowd by a white civil rights activist. Paralyzed and confined to a wheelchair, he ran for governor again in 1983, but this campaign was not a racist one. Wallace now wanted equality for blacks and received the support of Alabama's black leaders. He was victorious and fulfilled his promise to work for the betterment of all Alabamians, whatever their race.

A group of white people pour food and drink over these demonstrators holding a "sit-in" at a segregated food counter. The sit-in tactic was used throughout the South at places that refused to serve African Americans.

These events caused reverse crimes by African Americans. The worst example was the 1965 riots in the Watts district of Los Angeles. It began because a black driver was arrested, but one reason was the community's poverty and feeling of hopelessness. Up to 10,000 people rioted for six days, leaving 34 people dead, about 1,000 injured, and more than 4,000 arrested. Some 12,000 National Guardsmen were rushed there, but the rioters burned buildings and cars, causing $200 million in damages. In 1967, a riot by blacks killed 26 people and injured 1,500 in Newark, New Jersey, and another in Detroit killed 40 and injured about 2,000. After King's assassination the next year, more riots occurred in several cities, including Harlem in New York City.

Rosa Parks and the Civil Rights Movement

Rosa Parks was a quiet, dignified black woman who almost single-handedly began the civil rights movement. In 1955, she refused to sit in the back of a bus in Montgomery, Alabama, which the segregation law demanded.

Born Rosa Lee McCauley in 1913 in Tuskegee, Alabama, she became a seamstress and married Raymond Parks, a civil-rights activist. She served as the secretary of the Montgomery branch of the National Association for the Advancement of Colored People (NAACP). She was arrested after refusing a bus driver's order to give up her seat to a white man. Luckily, Martin Luther King, Jr. (see Chapter 3) was a young minister in the city at that time, and he organized a bus boycott, successfully challenging the law in a federal court.

Parks and her husband were fired from their jobs. She suffered from stress, and her husband had a nervous breakdown. They moved to Detroit, continuing to be active in civil rights, but had little money. In 1965, however, she began to work as secretary to Congressman John Conyers, Jr., of Michigan, and held this job until 1988. In 2000, on the

Rosa Parks' defiance of the bus segregation law in Montgomery, Alabama, led to a boycott that established Martin Luther King's, Jr.'s leadership in the civil rights movement.

Racial Crimes in the United States 39

45th anniversary of the bus boycott, she returned to Montgomery for the opening of the Rosa Parks Library and Museum. Two years later, her former apartment in Montgomery was placed on the National Register of Historic Places—a great tribute to her work.

The Civil Rights Act is Passed

The U.S. government did react strongly to the racist murders, African-American riots, and civil rights movement. In 1957, President Dwight Eisenhower sent in federal troops to guard black children entering a high school in Little Rock, Arkansas. President John F. Kennedy used Alabama National Guardsmen to protect the first two black students at the University of Alabama in 1963. Under President Lyndon Johnson's urging, Congress passed the Civil Rights Act of 1964 and the Voting Rights Act of 1965 to guarantee African-American and other minority rights. Those who opposed these laws were dealt with by the authorities.

School segregation is broken in Arkansas in 1957. President Dwight Eisenhower ordered the National Guard to protect African Americans enrolling at Little Rock High School, which had formerly admitted only white students.

One of the worst riots in U.S. history occurred in 1991, again in Los Angeles. Rodney King, a black motorist, was arrested for speeding, and four policemen beat him, an act filmed on video by a resident. When the policemen were tried and **acquitted** the following year, a four-day riot by blacks killed 55, injured 2,300, and caused $1 billion in damages. Two of the police were later convicted of violating King's civil rights and sent to prison for 30 months each. King received $3.8 million in compensation.

Racial and Ethnic Crimes Persist

Racially motivated crimes still occur on a fairly regular basis. The recent murders of Eric Garner, Michael Brown, and Walter Scott sparked nationwide protests against racially motivated police violence. Other examples include James Byrd, a black man, who was dragged behind a pickup truck outside Jasper, Texas. Three white men were convicted of the crime a year later, with two of them sentenced to die and one given life in prison. In another case, Buford Furrow, Jr., a racist, fired a gun into a Jewish Community Center in North Valley, California, wounding four children and a receptionist. He then shot and killed a Whittier mail carrier of Philippine origin. Furrow got life in prison. The 1990s also saw the burning and firebombing of many African-American churches throughout the South. Although racially motivated church burnings have fallen in recent years, 2009 (the most recent year for which statistics are available) counted nearly 120 cases.

The FBI's Hate Crime Statistics for 2012 shows that race was a factor in 46 percent of incidents. Blacks experience the most hate crime. The nation was shocked in 2015, when white racist Dylann Roof opened fire during a prayer service in a church in Charleston, South Carolina and killed nine black people, including state senator Clementa C. Pinckney. Roof claimed that he had done the shooting in hopes of starting a race war. This was sufficient motivation for South Carolina to finally remove the Confederate flag from the statehouse grounds, and most people claimed to have been appalled at the crime. Nonetheless, the Internet was also full of comments supporting Roof's act or at least the sentiments that motivated it.

Personal assault and damage to property are more common race crimes. After the September 11, 2001, terrorist attacks on the United States, attacks increased on Islamic and Asian students and buildings. This trend continued through the 2010s. As of 2015, hate crimes against Muslims in the United States remained high. The FBI estimated that there were about 150 anti-Islam hate crimes reported each year between 2001 and 2015, in contrast to the 20 or 30 crimes a year that occurred before 9/11 and the start of the War on Terror. According to the Bureau of Justice Statistics' National Crime Victimization Survey (NCVS), in 2012, an estimated 147,000 violent and property crimes were motivated by ethnicity.

In the mid-2010s racial tension seemed as bad as ever. Numerous riots occurred in Ferguson, Missouri, in 2014. This unrest was precipitated by the shooting of a black man, Michael Brown, by a white police officer. Police ended up establishing curfews and using riot squads to keep order, which only fueled the sense that police were unfairly targeting African Americans.

Demonstrators march in Ferguson, Missouri, protesting the shooting of Michael Brown by a white police officer.

Fighting Back Against Racism

Government agencies and many private and public organizations campaign against race and ethnic crimes. Besides maintaining the yearly Hate Crimes Statistics, the FBI investigates cases jointly with state and local law enforcement authorities. Following arrests, the FBI prosecutes for such crimes as murder, arson, and ethnic intimidation. Crimes investigated by the FBI are also prosecuted by the U.S. Department of Justice through the Criminal Section of its Civil Rights Division.

Equally active against racism are state and local government and law enforcement agencies. On the local level, for example, the Boston Police Department has created a Community Disorders Unit (CDU) to give special attention to racially motivated crimes. The Texas Civil Rights Project offers legal assistance to anyone who has experienced discrimination. After September 11, 2001, it created a Web site and hotline for Arabs and Muslims.

Among the best-known national organizations is the Southern Poverty Law Center in Montgomery, Alabama. This tracks race and hate groups, bringing legal cases against many. The Center for Democratic Renewal in Atlanta, Georgia, helps communities oppose racism and **bigotry**, linking hundreds of community groups around the nation that gather data on racial violence. In addition, the Anti-Defamation League fights **anti-Semitism** and other crimes of prejudice.

The FBI and Race Crimes

The FBI, part of the U.S. Department of Justice, is the primary federal agency that investigates race crimes. The FBI's role in racial crimes began with the passage of the Civil Rights Act in 1964. The first large case involved the murder of three civil rights workers in Mississippi that same year. The case was called MIBURN, which stood for Mississippi Burning (also the title of a 1988 movie about the FBI's investigation). In 1967, seven white men were convicted and received prison sentences.

Race violations are handled by the FBI's Civil Rights Program. The agency, as a member of the U.S. Attorney General's Hate Crimes Working Group, helped develop a national model to teach law enforcement officers and community members about crimes of prejudice. The FBI has also kept the nation's Hate Crime Statistics since Congress passed an act in 1990 requiring this. Today investigating hate crimes is the top priority of the Civil Right Program, both to protect people living in the United States and to prevent hate groups from inciting terrorism at home. The Matthew Shepard and James Byrd, Jr. Hate Crimes Prevention Act, passed in 2009, gives the federal government the authority to prosecute violent hate crimes and to aid state and local governments in their investigations and prosecutions of hate crimes. It also includes for the first time crimes motivated by hatred based on sexual orientation and gender identity. The Cold Case Initiative, created in 2007, allows FBI agents to reopen the cases of racially motivated killings from the civil rights era.

Text-Dependent Questions

1. What is the main racial problem in the United States?
2. What was segregation?
3. What was the civil rights movement?

Research Projects

1. Learn more about what happened to Native Americans when Europeans arrived, starting in the 1400s.
2. How did segregation work? What were some of the effects of this policy?
3. Learn more about the Ku Klux Klan, lynchings, and other forms of oppression used against blacks during the 20th century.

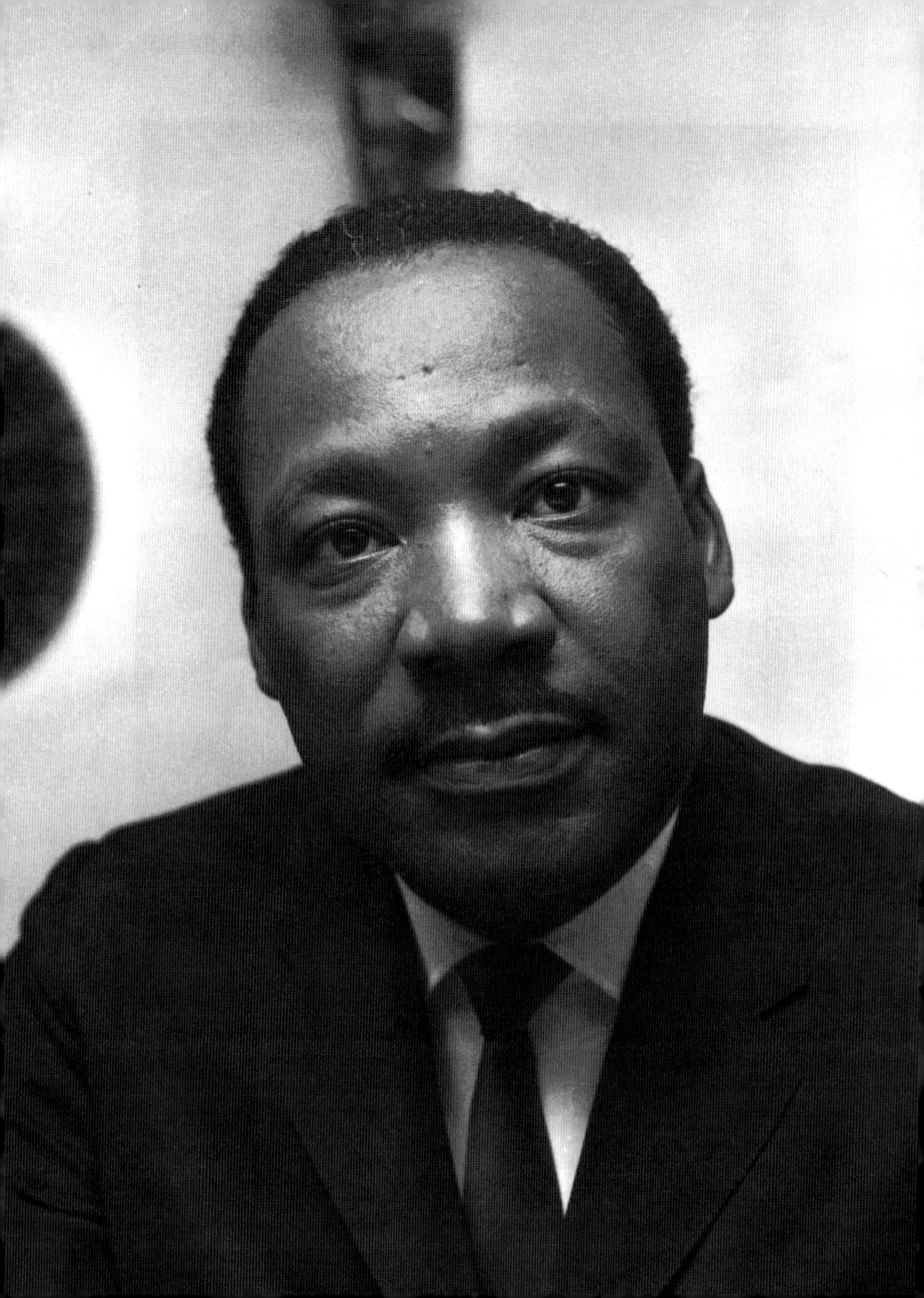

CHAPTER 3

DR. MARTIN LUTHER KING, JR.

Words to Understand

Civil disobedience: refusing, in a peaceful way, to obey a law
Desegregate: break down a system of segregation

WITHIN THE CIVIL RIGHTS MOVEMENT, THE CLERGYMAN MARTIN LUTHER KING, JR., WAS ALWAYS THE CENTRAL LEADER AND MAN OF PEACE. HE LED THE FIGHT FOR EQUAL RIGHTS WITHOUT VIOLENCE, TEACHING INSTEAD civil disobedience AND OTHER FORMS OF NONVIOLENT ACTION. DESPITE HIS NONVIOLENT APPROACH, HOWEVER, HE AND HIS FOLLOWERS BECAME THE VICTIMS OF MANY RACIST CRIMES, AND DR. KING'S CAMPAIGN FOR EQUAL RIGHTS WAS TRAGICALLY CUT SHORT WHEN HE WAS MURDERED. IN 1983, PRESIDENT RONALD REAGAN DECLARED THE THIRD MONDAY IN JANUARY A NATIONAL HOLIDAY, MARTIN LUTHER KING, JR. DAY. ALMOST EVERY MAJOR AMERICAN CITY NOW HAS A STREET OR SCHOOL NAMED AFTER HIM.

Martin Luther King, Jr., progressed from an unknown Baptist preacher to a world-famous leader who won the Nobel Peace Prize in 1964. His message of nonviolent protest won wide support from whites for the civil rights movement.

The First Victory of the Civil Rights Movement

King was born in 1929 in Atlanta, Georgia, the son of a Baptist minister. He earned degrees at Morehouse College in Atlanta and Crozier Theological Seminary in Chester, Pennsylvania, and then in 1955, received his Ph.D. degree in theology from Boston University. In 1954, King became the minister of the Dexter Avenue Baptist Church in Montgomery, Alabama, and the next year, the black woman Rosa Parks refused to give up her seat to a white man on a Montgomery city bus.

King, as head of the Montgomery Improvement Association, led a bus boycott that lasted 382 days and gained him national fame. He was a gifted speaker who could move the emotions of his listeners. During this time, he was arrested and his home bombed. However, the U.S. Supreme Court now ruled segregation was illegal on public transportation, and the Montgomery Bus Company had to let blacks sit anywhere on their buses. This was the first victory of the modern civil rights movement.

Martin Luther King, Jr. received extra strength from his wife, Coretta Scott King, and his family. In 1998, his son, Martin Luther King III (left), became head of the Southern Christian Leadership Conference that his father had founded.

Any civil rights protest became headline news when led by Martin Luther King, Jr. This interview took place in 1966, the year he began a campaign to end discrimination in Chicago's schools, housing, and workplaces.

King founded the Southern Christian Leadership Conference in 1957 as the base for his peaceful protests, marches, and demonstrations. He was elected president of the organization, and in the 11 years remaining in his life, he traveled more than six million miles, spoke over 2,500 times, and wrote five books, including *Why We Can't Wait* (1965). He was arrested 20 times and attacked four times.

In 1959, King and his wife, Coretta Scott King, whom he married in 1953, visited India, where he studied Mahatma Gandhi's nonviolent methods of protest.

Dr. Martin Luther King, Jr.

The next year, he moved to Atlanta to become co-pastor of the Ebenezer Baptist Church with his father, Martin Luther King, Sr. (His grandfather had also been pastor there.) Nine months later, the Atlanta police jailed him for taking part in a sit-in at a lunch counter.

"I Have a Dream"

King led a peaceful protest march in 1963 in Birmingham, Alabama, and the police responded by turning dogs and fire hoses on his followers. He was imprisoned for 11 days and on April 16, 1963, wrote his famous "Letter from a Birmingham Jail" explaining his campaign for black rights. On May 10, Birmingham dropped the charges and announced it would **desegregate** its schools, stores, and restaurants, and begin hiring more African Americans.

Martin Luther King, Jr. waves to the crowd gathered in front of the Lincoln Memorial in Washington, D.C. This was on August 28, 1963, when he delivered his now famous "I Have a Dream" speech during the "March on Washington."

The Life of Martin Luther King, Jr.

Despite dying at an early age, King helped bring about impressive changes in race relations in the United States. The following list outlines the major events in Martin Luther King, Jr.'s life:

1929: Born on January 15 in Atlanta, Georgia.

1944: Graduates from Booker T. Washington High School and enters Morehouse College at the age of 15.

1948: Ordained a Baptist minister at the age of 19; graduates from Morehouse College and enters Crozier Theological Seminary.

1951: Begins studies at Boston University.

1953: Marries Coretta Scott.

1954: Becomes minister of Dexter Avenue Baptist Church in Montgomery, Alabama.

1955: Leads Montgomery bus boycott to overturn segregation on buses.

1957: Forms the Southern Christian Leadership Conference.

1958: Stabbed in Harlem.

1959: Visits India with his wife to study nonviolent protests.

1960: Becomes co-pastor of Atlanta's Ebenezer Baptist Church with his father.

1963: Arrested in Birmingham, Alabama, and writes his "Letter from a Birmingham Jail"; leads a "Freedom Walk" of some 125,000 people in Detroit; leads the famous "March on Washington" with 250,000 participants.

1964: Awarded the Nobel Peace Prize in Oslo, Norway.

1965: Leads voting rights march from Selma to Montgomery, Alabama, protected by federal troops.

1966: Begins campaign in Chicago to end racial discrimination in schools, housing, and employment.

1967: Announces the "Poor People's Campaign."

1968: Leads march supporting sanitation workers in Memphis; gives his "I've Been to the Mountaintop" speech; assassinated a week later in Memphis.

President Lyndon Johnson shakes Martin Luther King, Jr.'s hand after signing the Civil Rights Act on July 2, 1964. The legislation came about largely because of King's impressive leadership in the campaign for equal rights.

In August, he led the March on Washington that brought about 250,000 people out onto the streets of the nation's capital to support new civil rights legislation. This was the largest civil rights demonstration in American history. It ended at the Lincoln Memorial on August 28, where King gave his famous speech. His words have gone down in history. He said, "I have a dream that my four children will one day live in a nation where they will not be judged by the color of their skin, but by the content of their character." Four months later, *Time* magazine named him "Man of the Year."

The march helped bring about the Civil Rights Act of 1964, the year King was awarded the Nobel Peace Prize, the youngest man to ever receive it. He donated the $54,123 award to the civil rights movement. That year, however, Black Muslims threw stones at him in Harlem. But King's message was winning, even though militants like Malcolm X and Stokely Carmichael urged blacks to reject King's tactics and to meet violence with violence. Also that year, King led a march in Alabama from Selma to Montgomery to increase voter registration for blacks, and President Lyndon B. Johnson signed the Voting Rights Act. In 1966, King began the "Poor Peoples Campaign" to help the poor of all races obtain both rights and jobs.

The Assassination of Martin Luther King, Jr.

At the age of 39, King was assassinated on April 4, 1968, in Memphis, Tennessee, where he was supporting local sanitation workers who were on strike. A week before in the city, he had led a march that turned violent, the first time this had ever happened. He was shot and killed while standing on a balcony of the Lorraine Motel. The night before, he had seemed to sense the end of his life, when he told his followers: "I would like to live a long life, longevity has its place, but I am not concerned about that now. I just want to do God's will. And He's allowed me to go up to the mountain, and I've looked over and I have seen the promised land. I may not get there with you, but I want you to know here tonight that we, as a people, will get to the promised land."

Riots and vandalism happened in many inner-city areas immediately after the assassination of Martin Luther King, Jr. Two months later, Robert Kennedy, another advocate for civil rights, was also assassinated.

The dream goes on as a young boy holds up an image of Dr. King during a parade marking Martin Luther King Jr. Day.

This violent death of one of the century's greatest civil rights leaders led to nationwide mourning and riots in 130 U.S. cities, with some 20,000 people arrested. James Earl Ray, the suspected killer, escaped to London, England, but was arrested there. The police found his fingerprints on a rifle and a pair of binoculars near the murder scene. He confessed to the murder in 1969 and was sentenced to 99 years in prison.

Not an Open-and-Shut Murder Case

James Earl Ray admitted he bought the rifle and rented a room in a rooming house facing the motel balcony. Days later, however, he said he was innocent and had given the gun to a man named "Raoul," who had set him up. Ray unsuccessfully asked for a retrial. In 1977, he escaped from the prison in Tennessee, but was recaptured three days later. The House Select Committee on Assassinations issued a report in 1978 saying other people were probably involved in the assassination, but did not name them.

Ray fought for years to have his name cleared. He argued that the police never ran a test to determine if the rifle was the one that had killed King. A Memphis bar owner claimed he was involved in the assassination plot. In 1996, a woman came forward saying she knew the man named Raoul, who was a weapons smuggler, and Ray's lawyer said he had tracked the man to the northeast. In 1997, one of King's sons, Dexter King, visited Ray to ask him point-blank if he had killed his father. When Ray said no, King said, "I believe you, and my family believes you, and we will do everything in our power to see you prevail." The Kings joined with Ray's family in requesting a new trial, but this was never granted. U.S. Attorney General Janet Reno ordered a review of the case in 1998, but Ray died that year in prison at the age of 70. King's family issued a statement saying it was "deeply saddened" by his death since a trial would have established the facts "concerning Mr. Ray's innocence." The review concluded in 2000 and found "no credible evidence" that others were involved in King's death.

James Earl Ray

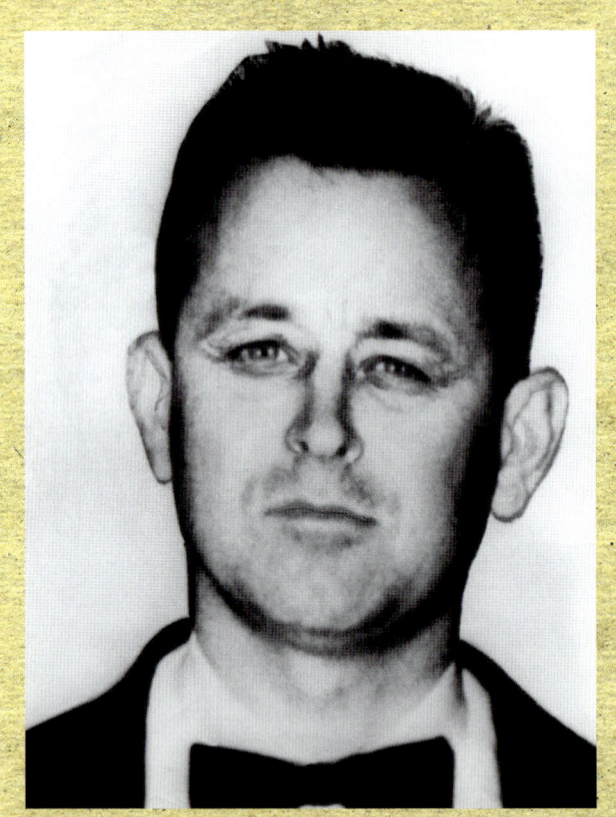

James Earl Ray, the convicted assassin of Martin Luther King, Jr., was born on May 10, 1929, in Alton, Illinois. He dropped out of high school and at the age of 16 took a job in a tannery. After being laid off, he enlisted in the Army in 1945 and was stationed in West Germany. He was discharged three years later for his lack of ability. He moved to California in 1949 and was arrested for robbing a cafe and sent to prison for 90 days.

Ray's criminal life continued. From 1952 to 1959, he served three different prison sentences for robbery. He was known as a loner in prison, and one inmate described him as a "not-too-bright hillbilly." However, Ray escaped from the Missouri State Penitentiary on April 23, 1967. A year later, when his fingerprints were found on a rifle near where Martin Luther King, Jr. was shot, the FBI identified Ray as the primary suspect.

He was arrested at Heathrow Airport in London, England, on June 8, 1968. Although Ray pleaded guilty and was sentenced to 99 years in prison, he spent the remaining 29 years of his life trying to clear his name.

Youth members of the Black Church Group march in in a Miami Martin Luther King, Jr. Day parade. The annual national holiday celebrating King's birthday is held on the third Monday in January.

Text-Dependent Questions

1. Who was Dr. Martin Luther King, Jr.?
2. What was the goal of the Southern Christian Leadership Conference?
3. How did King die?

Research Projects

1. January 15 was designated a federal holiday called Martin Luther King, Jr. Day in 1983. What were some of the controversies involved with creating this holiday and getting states to observe it?
2. Watch a video of King's "I Have a Dream" speech. Why was this speech so powerful?
3. How did King's civil rights movement operate? Why were peaceful protests so effective?

Dr. Martin Luther King, Jr.

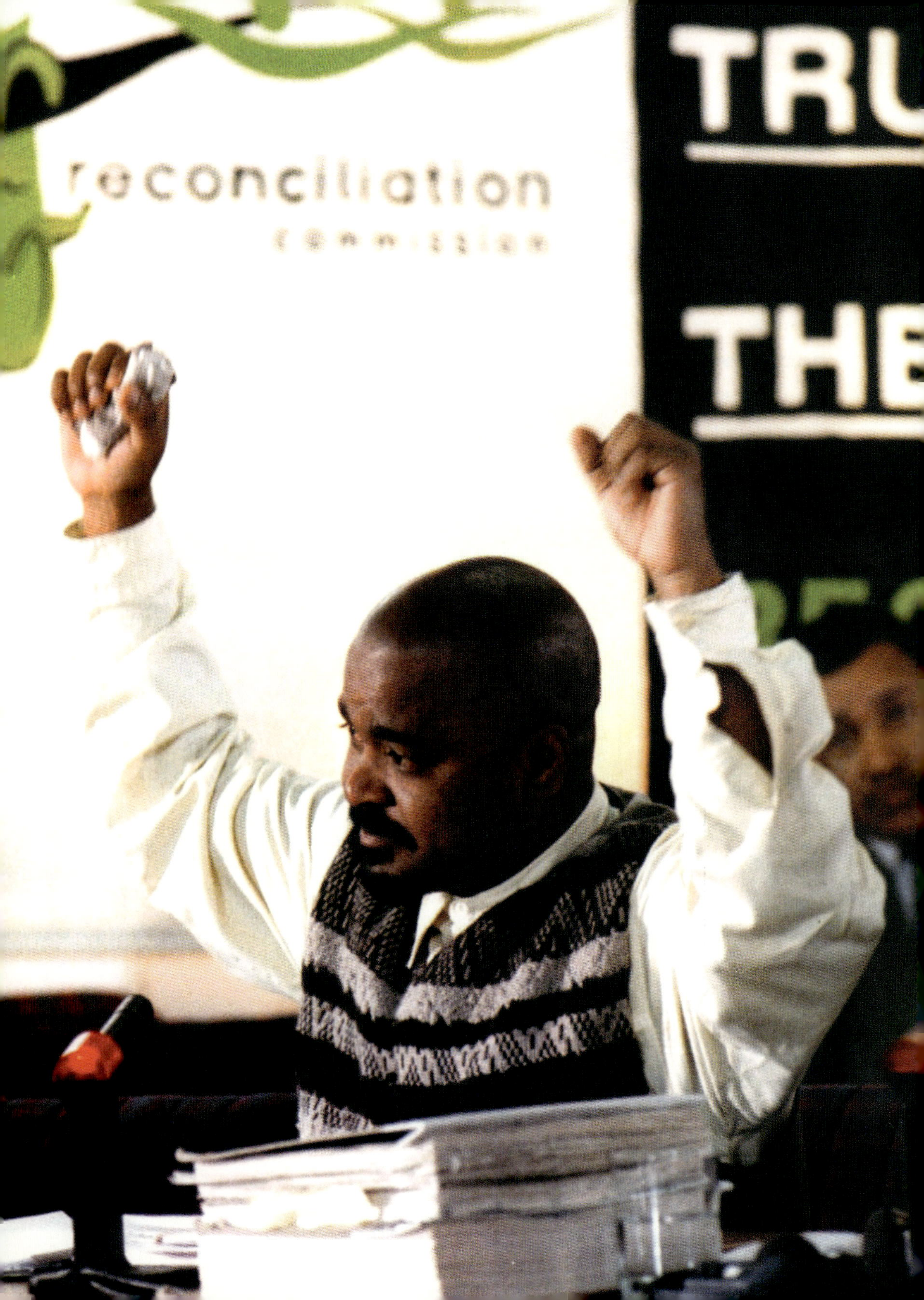
reconciliation
TRU
THE

CHAPTER 4

APARTHEID

Words to Understand

Activists: people who take an active role in political, social, or other matters

Amnesty: pardon given by a country to citizens who have committed crimes

Apartheid: a South African (Afrikaner) word meaning "apart-ness," it is the name for that nation's type of segregation

Embargo: a legal prohibition on commerce

Homelands: South African name for areas that blacks had to live on; these were also called Bantustans

Martyr: a person who sacrifices himself or herself for a cause

Sanctions: restrictive measures taken against a country by several other nations to make it change a policy, usually one that violates international law

APARTHEID (PRONOUNCED UH-PAR-TIDE) IS THE NAME USED IN SOUTH AFRICA FOR RACIAL SEGREGATION. IT IS GIVEN A SEPARATE CHAPTER BECAUSE SOUTH AFRICA WAS THE ONLY MAJOR COUNTRY IN THE 20TH CENTURY TO HAVE AN OFFICIAL NATIONWIDE SYSTEM TO SEPARATE THE RACES AND MAINTAIN WHITE SUPREMACY. IN THAT COUNTRY, 4.5 MILLION WHITES RULED THE MAJORITY OF 23 MILLION BLACKS.

The History and Background of Apartheid

South Africa is a beautiful, sweeping country of high plains, mountains, and deserts. It is home to several valuable minerals, being the world's largest exporter of gold and a major producer of diamonds. Uranium, iron, and copper are also mined. The many agricultural products include wine, fruit, sugar, corn, and wool.

Gary Kruser tells the Truth and Reconciliation Commission in South Africa how a policeman tortured him after he was captured as an African National Congress (ANC) guerrilla fighter in the late 1980s. Kruser was appointed a Deputy National Police Commissioner in 2016.

The richness of this land has lured Europeans for centuries. The first white settlers were the Dutch, who were called Boers, the Dutch word for farmers, in the 17th century. The British soon followed, establishing themselves in the south of the country. In 1899, the Boers rebelled against British rule and fought the colonial power for three years in the Anglo-Boer War. The British won, and they established the colony called the Union of South Africa. The Boers are now called Afrikaners. During these years of conflict, the Europeans kept control over the vastly larger native black population in order to keep the riches for themselves.

The South African Bureau for Racial Affairs coined the name apartheid, which means "apart-ness," in the 1930s. The country became independent from Britain in 1934. In the 1948 election, which it won, the Afrikaner National Party campaigned with a promise to make official the segregation that already existed and to extend it. The system also separated other races from one another, and these included "coloreds" (mixed race), "Asians" (mostly of Indian ancestry), and "Bantus" (African ancestry).

Like segregation in the South of the United States, apartheid separated the races in South Africa with many uncompromising laws. These black people had to sit on special benches for non-Europeans in a Johannesburg municipal park.

RACE AND CRIME

Under apartheid, blacks could hold only certain jobs, and they were paid far less than whites for the same work. They could not live in a white neighborhood or attend white schools. Only whites could vote and run for office. Marriages between the races were banned. Health services were hardly available to blacks, with there being only one black physician for every 44,000 blacks (but one white doctor for every 400 whites).

Categorizing Race

A Populations Registrations Act became law in 1950, forcing all South Africans to be registered as one of nine race types. In 1952, a system of "pass laws" made blacks carry identity papers in passbooks so the government could know where they were and restrict their movements. In 1953, separate public facilities were established for whites and nonwhites.

In 1959, a new policy of "separate development" created nine **homelands**, called "Bantustans," which put blacks, who made up 75 percent of the nation's population, on about 14 percent of the land. These areas were especially poor and unhealthy. The blacks had rights on these reservations, but few rights elsewhere. A black person without a passbook could be put in prison. (Compared to blacks, coloreds and Asians had a few limited rights.)

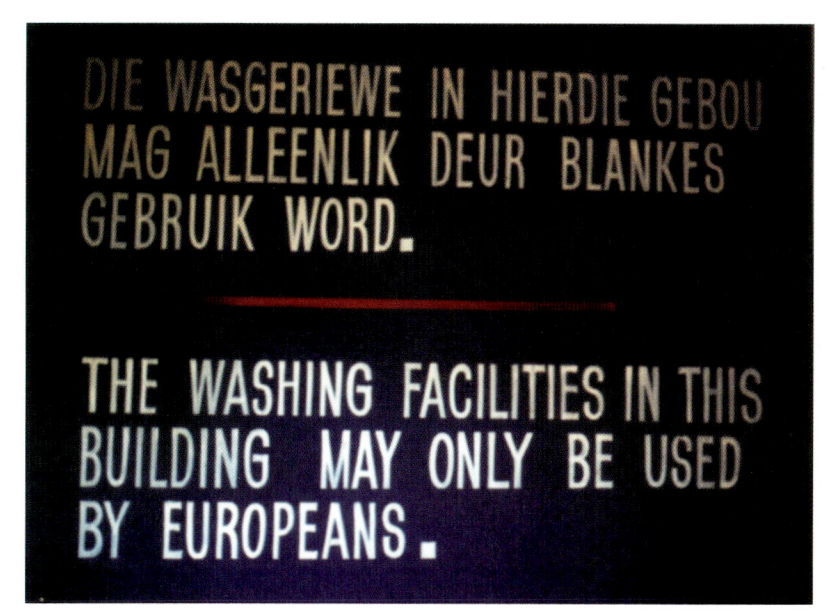

Stern warning signs during the apartheid era kept the best facilities for white Europeans. The warnings were posted in both English and the official language of Afrikaans, which is derived from a form of Dutch.

Opposition to Apartheid

In the 1950s, the main opposition to apartheid was the African National Congress (ANC), a political party established in 1912 to seek racial equality. It and other opposition groups were banned in 1960, and the ANC formed a militant wing led by Nelson Mandela. Resistance to racial crimes was brutally put down. At Sharpeville on March 21, 1960, government troops shot and killed 69 unarmed black people who were protesting the pass laws, and several thousand were arrested.

The massacre at Sharpeville on March 21, 1960, was one of the shocking events in the equal rights movement in South Africa. These bodies of protesters, including those of children, were gunned down by police officers.

Gandhi in South Africa

Mahatma Gandhi (1869–1948) is famous for his peaceful protests to gain India's independence from British rule. Less well-known is his earlier work in South Africa to remove racial discrimination against Indians. In 1893, he gave up his legal practice in Bombay, India, to work one year for a lawyer in South Africa. Traveling on a first-class ticket by train when he arrived, Gandhi was ordered to leave the car because colored people were not allowed in first class. He refused and was put out of the train on a freezing night.

Gandhi began working hard for Indian rights. When a law was passed that barred Indians from voting, he decided to stay in South Africa. He organized a political party and began a weekly newspaper. After many lost legal battles, however, he realized something more was needed. He developed a new "weapon" of passive resistance, which he called Satyagraha. The result was a serious improvement in rights for Indians.

In 1915, Gandhi finally returned to India and began the campaign that brought about independence. He was assassinated by a Hindu fanatic in 1948. Since then, several protest leaders, including Martin Luther King, Jr., have adopted his methods internationally.

Apartheid

Archbishop Desmond Tutu of Cape Town gives a friendly gesture during the Nelson Mandela Freedom Rally in Hyde Park in London, England, on July 17, 1988. This was on the eve of Mandela's 70th birthday. He was freed when he was 71 years old.

South Africa withdrew from the Commonwealth of Nations on May 31, 1961, because of apartheid and became the Republic of South Africa. In 1963, the United Nations suspended the country from the general assembly, and South Africa withdrew its UN ambassador. Mandela was arrested in 1964 and sentenced to life in prison after being charged with sabotage and trying to overthrow the government. In 1976, a student protest by students in the black township of Soweto resulted in 575 people killed over a period of eight months. The following year, the black civil rights leader Steve Biko was arrested and died in prison after being severely beaten by police.

Here, the forces of apartheid are apparent in 1992 when police fire on the marching residents of Alexandria Township. Since the fall of apartheid in 1994, many officers have confessed their crimes to the Truth and Reconciliation Commission and been given **amnesty** against prosecution.

Apartheid

Nelson Mandela

Nelson Mandela could be called South Africa's Martin Luther King, Jr. because he led his people to freedom and equality. However, Mandela went beyond King's peaceful resistance to oppose the brutal South African government. He was a brave fighter who suffered a long imprisonment from 1964 to 1982. His reputation grew, however, and he became a symbol of resistance to apartheid.

Mandela was born on July 18, 1918, in the village of Qunu. He was chosen by the chief of Thembuland to be groomed for high office, but chose to begin a BA degree at the University College of Fort Hare, which educated colored students in the Eastern Cape town of Alice. Mandela was expelled for joining a protest boycott and went to Johannesburg to complete the degree by correspondence.

In 1942, he joined the African National Congress and traveled the country, organizing resistance to apartheid laws. When the ANC was banned in 1960, Mandela went underground to lead the military wing in a campaign of sabotage against the government. In 1962, he went to Algeria for military training. He was arrested when he returned and in the same year he was sentenced to five years in jail. While in prison, he was also convicted of sabotage and for this he was given a life sentence.

In prison, Mandela remained a dignified man and was a source of strength for other prisoners. In the 1970s and 1980s, he refused offers of freedom if he would renounce violence. When he was finally released in 1990, however, he immediately ended the ANC's armed struggle. Four years later, he was elected president of his country. At his inauguration, Mandela dedicated the day to "all the heroes and heroines in this country and the rest of the world who sacrificed in many ways and surrendered their lives so that we could be free." And he added: "The time to build is upon us. We pledge ourselves to liberate all our people from the continuing bondage of poverty, deprivation, suffering, gender, and other discrimination."

In 1986, riots and strikes forced the government to declare a national state of emergency. The government's security forces were given almost unlimited powers, and restrictions were put on press reports. That same year, the South African bishop, Desmond Tutu, who had won the Nobel Peace Prize, asked Western nations to put **sanctions** on South African trade to pressure the nation to give up apartheid. Sports teams from many countries would not play South African teams, and entertainers from other countries refused to perform there.

The pressures worldwide and at home brought results. The term "apartheid" was replaced with "plural democracy." President P.W. Botha ended the ban on interracial marriages in 1985, and the next year, when the U.S. Congress imposed strict economic sanctions against South Africa, the pass laws were abolished.

F. W. de Klerk Reverses the Laws of Apartheid

When about two million black workers in South Africa held a nationwide strike in 1988, President Botha resigned and was replaced by F. W. de Klerk. The next year, the new president desegregated all public facilities and released the imprisoned ANC **activists**. De Klerk then freed Nelson Mandela (after 27 years in prison) on February 11, 1990, and legalized the ANC and 32 other opposition groups. A year later, black students entered previously all-white public schools, and de Klerk ended all of the apartheid laws and called for a new constitution. U.S. president George Bush also lifted most of the economic sanctions against South Africa. In 1992, the whites of South Africa went to the polls and 70 percent voted to end their minority rule.

In 1993, the United States and the United Nations lifted their remaining economic sanctions, South Africa abolished the homelands and established a temporary multiracial "government of national unity," and de Klerk and Mandela were jointly awarded the Nobel Peace Prize. Accepting the award, Mandela said it was a call "that we devote what remains of our lives to the use of our country's unique and painful experience to demonstrate that human existence should be based on democracy, prosperity, and solidarity."

Soweto

South Africa's largest township during apartheid was Soweto, which is short for South-Western Townships (several are combined). In 1948, the government set aside the 25 square miles (65 sq km) of land with its tiny houses for workers living outside Johannesburg. On June 16, 1976, about 15,000 schoolchildren joined a march to protest a new requirement that classes be taught in the Afrikaans language of their rulers. The peaceful demonstration turned violent, and people disagree about which side attacked first. The police fired into the crowd and killed 130 people, including children. Outrage was felt by blacks throughout the country, leading to riots and 575 deaths.

Soweto had been the home of Nelson Mandela and Bishop Desmond Tutu. When Mandela returned there in 2000, he paid tribute to the youths who were "mowed down by apartheid bullets," saying he had gained inspiration from their courage. Today, Soweto is overcrowded, with about two million people living in poverty. Violence and crime are daily occurrences. Still, many tourists visit Soweto to see the township that helped weaken the apartheid system. As Mandela told the residents: "Your struggles, your commitment, and your discipline have released me to stand here before you today."

Nelson Mandela and South African president F. W. de Klerk pose with their Nobel Peace Prizes, awarded in 1993 in Oslo, Norway. The two men shared the prestigious prize for their cooperative work to end apartheid.

Mandela was elected president the following year when his ANC party gained two-thirds of the vote in the first election open to all races. During the political campaigning, racists tried to interrupt the election by carrying out bombings in the cities of Johannesburg and Pretoria. In 1994, South Africa's membership in the Commonwealth was restored. President Mandela appointed a Truth and Reconciliation Commission in 1995 to record the human rights abuses that had occurred under apartheid. People who confessed their racial crimes were given amnesty. The new constitution became law the following year.

The Lessons Of Apartheid

Something good finally did come from apartheid. It confirmed the existence of a strong international dislike of racism and showed that worldwide cooperation can defeat racial prejudice. Even those who practiced apartheid turned against it. "We wanted to get off the tiger," said F. W. de Klerk, "but we didn't want to get devoured by the tiger when we got off."

Speaking at Harvard University in 2001, de Klerk compared apartheid to segregation in the United States and urged people to learn the lessons of the past, but to face the future. He said, "If we continue to spend too much energy arguing the past, we lose the window to see the future. I'm not asking to forget the past. But, when you focus exclusively on the past, you sow the seeds for new tensions. We need to close the past, to a certain extent, without forgetting, so that it doesn't hold us down from doing what we need to do in the future."

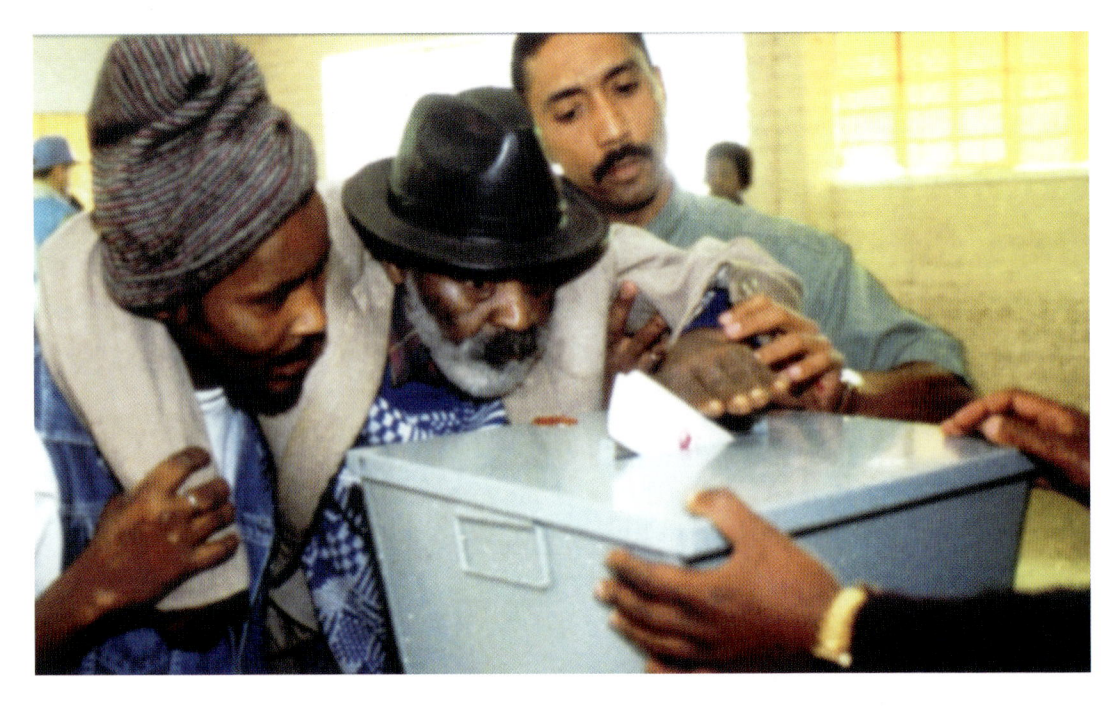

A 75-year-old invalid, who lived in a squatter camp outside Cape Town, is helped to cast his vote on April 26, 1994. In this first South African election in which all races could vote, Nelson Mandela was elected president.

Steve Biko

Steve Biko has been called the greatest **martyr** of the anti-apartheid movement. Born in 1946 in Eastern Cape, South Africa, the intelligent youth was accepted into the "Black Section" of the University of Natal Medical School. He gave up his medical study to fight against apartheid and in 1969, founded the Black Consciousness Movement.

He promoted black pride and told blacks to stop feeling inferior to whites. He said blacks should not work with whites for equality because whites would not help them. His harsh words even caused a break with the African National Congress. The government began restricting his movements in 1973 and would not let him be quoted in any publication or through any other form of media.

Biko was arrested five times, the last being on August 21, 1977. He died on September 12, 1977, of head wounds sustained while in police custody. The world was shocked when South Africa's Minister of Justice said, "Biko's death leaves me cold." However, his brutal death caused a worldwide outcry, and the United States and many other countries soon imposed an oil and arms **embargo** on South Africa.

The police first claimed Biko had died while on a hunger strike, but later claimed he hit his head on a wall during a scuffle with police officers. In 1997, five policemen finally confessed to the Truth and Reconciliation Commission that they had beaten Biko, but added that they did not think that this caused his death. The commission granted amnesty to the policemen, since this would encourage others to confess the truth.

Biko's life story was the subject of Richard Attenborough's 1987 movie *Cry Freedom*, with Denzel Washington portraying the freedom fighter. In 1997, on the 20th anniversary of his death, President Nelson Mandela unveiled a bronze statue of Biko. Mandela called him "one of the greatest sons of our nation" and quoted Biko's famous words: "In time, we shall be in a position to bestow on South Africa the greatest possible gift—a more human face."

The black activist Steve Biko was arrested five times during his last years and then died in police custody after being beaten. His inspirational words and life of self-sacrifice have made him the hero of many black Africans.

Text-Dependent Questions

1. What is apartheid?
2. Who are the Afrikaners?
3. When did apartheid end?

Research Projects

1. Who was Mahatma Gandhi? What role did he have in developing racial tolerance in South Africa? What else did he do?
2. Who was Nelson Mandela? What are some of his many accomplishments?
3. Why did white South Africans refuse to end apartheid for so many years? What made them finally capitulate?

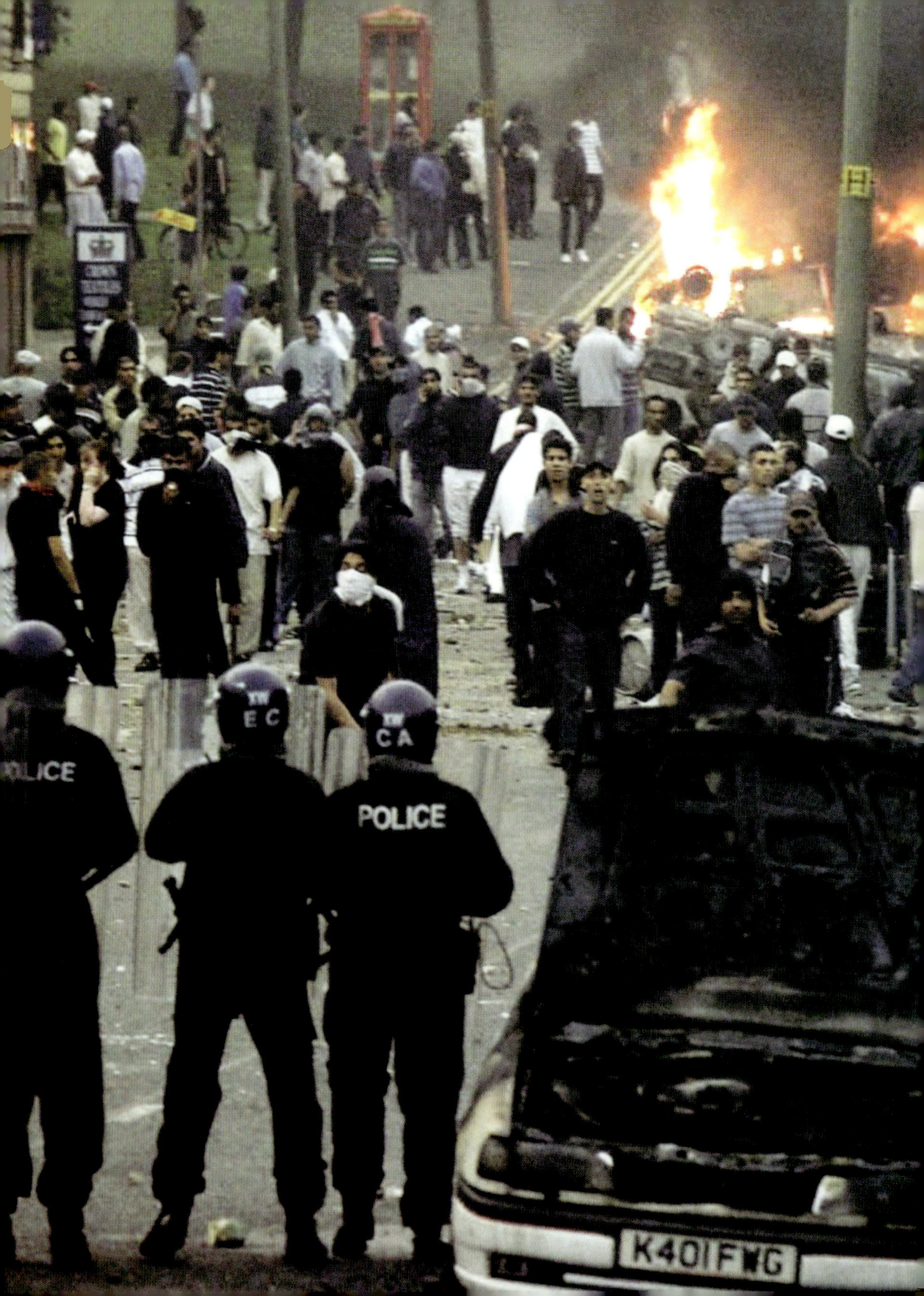
E C
C A
POLICE
K401FWG

CHAPTER 5

RACE CRIMES IN OTHER NATIONS

Words to Understand

Molotov cocktails: explosive weapons; each "cocktail" is a bottle filled with gasoline and wrapped in a rag or plugged with a wick, then ignited and thrown

Skinhead: young person, usually a racist, who has a short haircut (or a shaved head) and wears heavy boots

Xenophobia: fear of foreigners or foreign things

A DISTURBING TREND IN THE EARLY 21ST CENTURY IS THE INCREASE OF RACE CRIMES IN EUROPE AND OTHER AREAS OF THE WORLD. AS IN THE UNITED STATES, LEADERS OF RACIST ORGANIZATIONS ARE DRESSING RESPECTABLY AND SOUNDING MORE EDUCATED TO ATTRACT A GREATER FOLLOWING. THE RACIST BRITISH NATIONAL PARTY, FOR EXAMPLE, WAS DESCRIBED AS "RACE HATE IN A SUIT" BY READER'S DIGEST. ANTI-BLACK PROPAGANDA HAS BECOME ANTI-IMMIGRANT THROUGHOUT EUROPE, WHICH HAS GAINED SOME EXTREMIST PARTIES ENOUGH VOTES TO ELECT MEMBERS TO NATIONAL LEGISLATIVE BODIES.

British police face Asian youths while cars burn in some of the worst rioting experienced in Britain in recent years. Racial tension led to rioting and battles between far-right extremists and Asian youth in Burnley, Bradford, and Oldham in the north of England in the summer of 2001.

South Africa's retired bishop Desmond Tutu warned in 2002 that racism can never be conventional and acceptable. Speaking to the Episcopal Divinity School in Cambridge, Massachusetts, he reminded us that, "it is racism that resulted in the awfulness of lynchings and the excesses of slavery; it spawned the Holocaust and apartheid and was responsible for ethnic cleansing."

Racism Rears its Ugly Head in Europe

European racism was highlighted in the 2002 national election in France when Jean-Marie Le Pen of the National Front received the second largest amount of votes (although he was defeated badly by President Jacques Chirac). Millions protested in the streets against Le Pen's surprising popularity, which was helped by the voters' boredom with the other parties. France has many Arab immigrants, and Le Pen has called for an end to legal immigration, the deportation of illegal immigrants, and restrictions on giving French citizenship to foreigners. He even downplayed the killing of six million Jews during the Holocaust by calling this "a point of detail in the history of the Second World War."

Jean-Marie Le Pen, the extreme-right National Front party leader, gestures to supporters during a campaign rally in Marseille on May 2, 2002. He was beaten in the final round by President Jacques Chirac.

Demonstrations against Jean-Marie Le Pen broke out in France following his surprise first-round defeat of the socialist French prime minister Lionel Jospin on April 21, 2002. Thousands marched through Paris and other cities. This group marched with posters proclaiming, "youth against the extreme right."

Race Crimes in Other Nations 75

The Austrian Freedom Party

In 2000, for the first time in history, the European Union (EU) put sanctions on one of its members. This happened after the anti-immigration Austrian Freedom Party (FPO) won 27 percent of the vote in the 1999 parliamentary elections, making it the country's second strongest party. The FPO was headed by Jorg Haider (pictured), the governor of the Austrian state of Carinthia. He addressed a meeting of Austrian veterans of Hitler's brutal specialist forces, the SS, saying they had suffered during the war. He also praised Hitler's employment program and called Nazi concentration camps "punishment camps."

The other 14 members of the EU froze diplomatic contacts with Austria and imposed other sanctions for letting the FPO join a coalition government. Haider took back his comments and called for better treatment of ethnic minorities in Europe. He even asked for compensation for slave laborers exploited by Hitler's regime. After receiving more criticism for visiting Iraq's president, Saddam Hussein, in 2000, he resigned as head of the party. The EU then removed its sanctions, which had been in place for seven months. Haider remained governor of Carinthia and even visited Iraq again in 2002 to express Austria's "solidarity" with Iraq.

The FPO regained its power under the leadership of chairman Heinz-Christian Strache during the 2000s, to the point that by 2011 its support in opinion polls was around 25 percent–and much higher among people under 30. The party seeks to promote Austrian cultural identity and to end immigration. This was an increasingly touchy subject as of 2015 due to the large number of migrants from Syria and the rest of the Middle East passing through Austria on their way to other European destinations.

RACE AND CRIME

Demonstrators in the Austrian capital of Vienna make their opposition to Jorg Haider known at a rally in May 2002. Police had to seal off part of the city to avoid potential clashes between antifascists and far-right supporters marking the anniversary of the capitulation of Nazi Germany.

Race Crimes in Other Nations

Le Pen's surprising vote came at a time when anti-Semitism was on the rise across Europe. This was fueled by the Israeli-Palestinian conflict, and many of the suspects were Arabs. During two weeks in France in 2002, a total of 360 anti-Semitic incidents were recorded. One school bus taking Jewish children to school was attacked on three different occasions. More than five million Muslims live in France, compared with 475,000 Jews, and the two groups often live together in housing projects, like those in the Paris suburbs.

International Jewish leaders warned that the level of attacks in Europe was the highest since World War II, with Jews attacked in Germany, Belgium, and Russia. Synagogues were firebombed in several French cities and Jewish cemeteries vandalized in several countries. The World Council of Churches noted the increase in the number of recorded racial crimes associated with neo-Nazi groups in Germany and Sweden, and it began a new project called "Churches in Europe: Initiatives to Overcome Racism, **Xenophobia**, and Racial Violence."

Other leaders of racist or extreme nationalist political parties in Europe have caused concern in Austria, Italy, Switzerland, Belgium, Denmark, and The Netherlands. In The Netherlands, Pim Fortuyn argued that immigrants, especially from Islamic countries, would, in the long term, threaten his nation's liberal traditions. He sought to limit immigration, and was expected to receive up to 20 percent of the vote in the 2002 legislative election. Sadly, he was assassinated two weeks before the election.

The problem has not improved over the years. By the mid-2010s, crimes based on race and religion were surging in Europe. Anti-Semitism, anti-Muslim, and anti-Roma attacks are particular problems. In times of economic hardship, racist politicians can foment resentment against particular groups, which can lead to violent attacks on them and their businesses. There were 47,210 racist crimes reported across the European Union in 2013, with Muslims, blacks, and Roma the most frequent victims. Muslim women are particularly vulnerable to attacks by men. This is an increase over previous years, and corresponds with the rise in far-right political parties and hate speech by politicians, influenced by conflict in Israel and Palestine and by Muslim terrorist attacks that raise fears in Europe and around the world. A Muslim terrorist attack on the French satirical magazine *Charlie Hebdo* in 2015 precipitated rallies and demonstrations around the world, supporting both the victims and the attackers. Anti-Semitism is also on the rise, so much so that in 2015 a number of observers actually questioned whether it might be time for Jews to leave France entirely for their own safety.

Le Pen's daughter Marine Le Pen took over leadership of the National Front in 2011 and tried to steer the party away from racism and anti-Semitism, though the party remains staunchly anti-immigration and socially conservative. Mr. Le Pen protested vigorously, but the National Front expelled him in 2015.

Racial Tensions in Britain

Britain has probably worried about racism in its country longer than its neighbors in Europe and it has one of the highest rates of racial violence in Western Europe. Many immigrants from its Commonwealth nations were able to settle in Britain after World War II, but they were often crowded into poor urban areas.

Racial violence flared up in 1958 in London's Notting Hill area between whites and blacks after a group of white men attacked a white Swedish woman married to a West Indian. Large riots happened in 1981 in Brixton in south London, a multicultural area where many blacks and Asians live. The rioters blamed the police's new policy of stopping and searching black youths. More than 300 people were injured, including more than 200 police officers, and the damage to buildings and vehicles was estimated at £7.5 million (about $12 million).

In 1995, Asian youths rioted in Bradford in West Yorkshire, throwing **Molotov cocktails** and rocks at riot police, breaking store windows, and setting cars on fire. Bradford

Police watched as gasoline-bombed cars burned after the rioting in the Brixton district of London, England. Local residents blamed the riots on the police, accusing them of discriminating against black youths.

again had racial rioting in 2001, as did Oldham, an industrial town in Greater Manchester in northwest England, where Asian youths fought battles in the streets after whites attacked Asian homes. Nearly 100 people were arrested after causing thousands of pounds of damage.

In 2011, 87 percent of the U.K. population was white, a decrease from 92 percent in 2001. Of the rest, 7 percent was Asian or Asian British, 3 percent was black or black British, and about two percent mixed. The decreasing proportion of whites is one reason for racial tension. Racism has been reported in many aspects of society, including the workplace, theater, universities, and at soccer games. The worst charges have been against the respected British bobby (police), and cities are setting up programs to let victims of racial crimes report them to a counselor at a civil center or other building, to remove the fear of entering a police station.

The Murder of Stephen Lawrence

The brutal London murder of Stephen Lawrence, an 18-year-old black man, resulted in Britain's longest-running investigation into a race crime, and the case became the driving force to improve race relations and eliminate racial prejudice in the police department.

Stephen Lawrence was a Boy Scout who had wanted to be an architect since he was seven years old, and he already had a job offer from a local architect. Stephen and his friend, Duwayne Brooks, were rushing to catch a bus in the London suburb of Eltham when a gang of white youths attacked them. Duwayne escaped, but Stephen ran only 200 yards before he collapsed and died. The police arrived within minutes, but their later investigation was weak and half-hearted. Blacks said this was because the police had little interest in conducting an aggressive investigation into whites killing a black.

Stephen's parents, who had immigrated to Britain from Jamaica in the 1960s, launched their own private prosecution, but it collapsed. In the meantime, five white suspects were arrested, but the police had not collected enough evidence to hold them, even though they had installed a secret video camera in one suspect's apartment, which showed the group waving knives and expressing racist views.

In 1997, an investigation by the Police Complaints Authority found no racist conduct by the police, just a weakness in the investigation. However, the government began an independent investigation that year, led by Sir William Macpherson. In 1999, the Macpherson Report said there was institutional racism in the London police force and other forces around the nation. It decided this was not done on purpose, but was due to attitude, thoughtlessness, and racist stereotyping. The

Police stand next to a poster raised by the Stephen Lawrence Family Campaign. This photograph was taken on June 29, 1998, during the official inquiry into the murder in London. The final report led to changes in the way police handle race cases.

Race Crimes in Other Nations

Macpherson Report made 70 recommendations on breaking down racism, and the British government accepted all of them. The police responded by forming a Racial and Violent Crime task force.

Keeping Track of Race Crime

The Institute of Race Relations in London keeps track of racist incidents and hate crimes that take place in the United Kingdom In 2011–12 people in England and Wales reported 47,678 racist incidents to the police. That amounted to an average of about 130 racist incidents a day. During the same time, there were 35,816 reported race hate crimes and 1,621 religious hate crimes. Police believe that racial violence is underreported, and suspected that the real number of racially motivated hate crimes was closer to 130,000.

There were even some murders. Between 1993 and 2013 there were 105 deaths that the IRR attributed to race. Most of these murders were attacks in the street, and 20 of them targeted taxi drivers, shopkeepers, and pub employees at work.

Neo-Nazis in Russia

Russia should be one of the last countries to have a neo-Nazi movement. Hitler's Nazi troops invaded Russia during World War II, a conflict that cost three million lives alone during the siege of Leningrad (now St. Petersburg). Today's neo-Nazi Russians, however, have turned their violence primarily against blacks and other colored people, but also against any foreigners, including Americans. The movement began in the early 1990s, and some estimates say there are now more than 30,000 neo-Nazis in Russia, most members being of high-school age.

Their acts of intimidation and violence are common. A black U.S. Marine, who was a security guard at the U.S. embassy, was beaten by neo-Nazis in 1998. On March 15, 2001, 20 neo-Nazis attacked a Moscow school for Armenian students, in which several students were badly beaten. In April 2002, when the racist organizations celebrated Hitler's birthday, a neo-Nazi group sent an e-mail to the Indian embassy, ordering all Indians to leave Russia and saying they would kill all foreigners because "Russia is for Russians." Although the Russian police has battled against the movement, few crimes have gone to court.

A demonstrator held an Israeli flag while protesting in front of the European Parliament in Brussels to an end to anti-Semitic attacks.

Britain's leading racist political party is the British National Party (BNP), which has an estimated membership of 3,000. The party's slogan is "Defend Rights for Whites," and it calls for a "voluntary resettlement" of blacks and Asians. The BNP's membership declined between 2010 and 2015. Other racist groups include the National Front, White Wolves, implicated in some bomb plots, and the neo-Nazi Combat 18, which is suspected of several murders.

Racism and racial attacks are also problems in other European nations, which have experienced a rise in **skinhead** and neo-Nazi groups. The increase in worldwide racial violence is primarily linked to increased immigration, the September 11, 2001 terrorist attacks on the United States, and the Israeli-Palestinian conflict. Muslim terrorism of the 2000s and 2010s has increased prejudices against Muslims, resulting in some violent attacks on them. Historical prejudices also remain in many areas, like Serbia, Bosnia, and Kosovo.

Racial hate crimes are believed to be on the rise in numerous countries, including Finland, Spain, Italy, Sweden, and many other countries. Anti-Semitism is a particular problem, but racial animosity extends to other groups as well. In 2014 and 2015 large numbers of migrants from other parts of the world attempted to move into and through Europe, causing a reaction among the inhabitants who worried that white Europe was being overrun. In Russia, targets of racism include Jews, Muslims from the Causasus, and blacks. Neo-Nazi gangs have been convicted for attacking and murdering foreigners.

Race Crimes in Other Nations

Germany has experienced its own resurgence in racism in the 2010s, with the appearance of neo-Nazi groups. Swastikas have been spray-painted onto buildings. German gangs have firebombed the homes of Turkish workers, and France has experienced violence against the five million Muslims living there. Spain has seen more racial crimes against immigrants from African nations, especially Algeria and Morocco. The Roma or Gypsies, also called the Travelers, are ubiquitous in Europe and are almost universally either attacked or ignored by most Europeans, especially in Central and Eastern Europe.

Racial Violence in Africa and Elsewhere

Africa itself has seen blacks attacking white farmers and others who once ruled their nations. The worst violence has been in Zimbabwe, where President Robert Mugabe began encouraging blacks to take over white farms which resulted in a number of murders and beatings of the white owners and their black workers. White farmers have also been attacked in South Africa to drive them off the land, and white racist crimes continue despite the end of apartheid. In 2000, a white man tied his black employee to the back of his pickup truck and dragged him to death.

Racial problems run deep in Africa, though. The nation of Mauritania only outlawed slavery in 2007, though many blacks are believed to still be enslaved to Arabs. Slavery is also practiced in Niger. Racial and ethnic conflict have produced violence in Nigeria, Somalia, Ethiopia, and Eritrea. The 1994 genocide in Rwanda was motivated in part by ethnic differences.

Asian racial conflict receives less news space in the West, but is still extensive. In Indonesia, there has been much violence against the rich Indonesian-Chinese minority, who are blamed for economic problems, and many Cambodians are anti-Vietnamese. China and Japan have resented one another for centuries. China and India both have ancient social divisions that persist to this day, resulting in significant discrimination. In India, the Dalit or "Untouchables" are particularly likely to be the victims of violent crimes such as gang rapes.

UN Efforts to Combat Racism

The upswing in race crimes and racist groups, however, has been met by a worldwide increase in cooperative programs and plans to combat these groups and their crimes. The UN's World Conference on Racism in 2001 was such a meeting, producing heated opinions and walk-outs, but also a declaration against racism. The UN held another conference against racism in Geneva in 2009. The UN also has a created a treaty, the International Convention on the Elimination of All Forms of Racial Discrimination, which took effect in 1969. Member states promise to eliminate racial discrimination, outlaw hate speech, criminalize membership in racist organizations, and promote understanding among all races. By 2013, 177 nations were party to this convention.

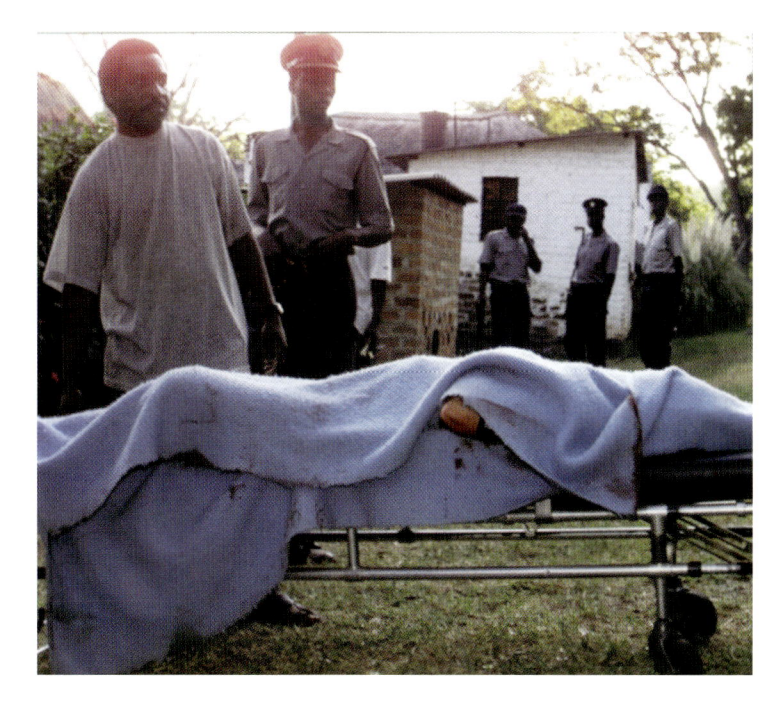

Here, Zimbabwean policemen wait to take away the body of a murdered white farmer from a farming estate outside Harare. Racial tensions in Zimbabwe led to the deaths of many white farmers as their farms were invaded by supporters of Robert Mugabe.

Text-Dependent Questions

1. What is the National Front?
2. What is anti-Semitism?
3. What are skinheads and neo-Nazis?

Research Projects

1. Investigate anti-Semitism in Europe. How long have Jews been persecuted? What are some of the things that have happened to them over the centuries?
2. What immigration trends are causing racial tensions in Europe to increase?
3. Who are the Roma, or Gypsies? Why are they so often targets of racism?

Race Crimes in Other Nations   85

SERIES GLOSSARY

Amnesty: pardon given by a country to citizens who have committed crimes

Anarchist: a person who wants to do away with organized society and government

Antiglobalization: against large companies or economies spreading into other nations

Appeal: referral of a case to a higher court for review

Arraignment: a formal court hearing at which the prisoner is asked whether he or she pleads "guilty" or "not guilty" to the charge or charges

Bifurcated: divided into two branches or parts

Bioassay: chemical analysis of biological samples

Biometrics: use of physical characteristics, such as fingerprints and voice, to identify users

Certificate of certiorari: a document that a losing party files with the Supreme Court, asking the Supreme Court to review the decision of a lower court; it includes a list of the parties, a statement of the facts of the case, and arguments as to why the court should grant the writ

Circumstantial evidence: evidence that can contribute to the conviction of an accused person but that is not considered sufficient without eyewitness or forensic evidence

Civil disobedience: refusing, in a peaceful way, to obey a government policy or law

Clemency: an act of leniency or mercy, especially to moderate the severity of punishment due

Commute: to change a penalty to another one less severe

Cryptology: the science and art of making and breaking codes and ciphers

Dactylography: the original name for the taking and analysis of fingerprints

Deputy: a person appointed as a substitute with power to act

Dissident: someone who disagrees with an established religious or political system, organization, or belief

Distributed Denial of Service (DDOS) attack: a malware attack that floods all the bandwidth of a system or server, causing the system to be unable to service real business

Effigy: a model or dummy of someone

Electronic tagging: the attaching of an electronic device to a criminal after he or she has been released, in order to track the person to ensure that he or she does not commit a crime again

Ethics: the discipline dealing with what is good and bad and with moral duty and obligation

Euthanasia: the act of killing or permitting the death of hopelessly sick or injured individuals in a relatively painless way for reasons of mercy

Exhume: to dig up a corpse, usually for examination

Exoneration: a finding that a person is not in fact guilty of the crime for which he or she has been accused

Extortion: the act of obtaining money from a person by force, intimidation, or undue or illegal power

Forensics: the scientific analysis and review of the physical and medical evidence of a crime

Garrote: to strangle someone using a thin wire with handles at either end

Gibbet: an upright post with a projecting arm for hanging the bodies of executed criminals as a warning

Graft: the acquisition of gain (as money) in dishonest or questionable ways

Grievance: a real or imagined wrong, for which there are thought to be reasonable grounds for complaint

Heresy: religious convictions contrary to church dogma and that deviate from orthodox belief

Hulk: a ship used as a prison

Hypostasis: the migration of blood to the lowest parts of a dead body, caused by the effect of gravity

Incendiary: a bomb

Infiltrate: to enter or become established in gradually or unobtrusively, usually for subversive purposes

Intern (v.): to confine or impound, especially during a war

Interpol: an association of national police forces that promotes cooperation and mutual assistance in apprehending international criminals and criminals who flee abroad to avoid justice

Intrusion detection system (IDS): software designed to detect misuse of a system

Junta: a group of military officers who hold power, usually as the result of a coup

Jurisprudence: a system or body of law

Ladder: an early form of the rack in which the victim was tied to a vertical framework and weights were attached to his ankles

Lag: a convict

Latent: present and capable of becoming obvious, or active, even though not currently visible

Lockstep: a mode of marching in step where people move one after another as closely as possible

Lynch: to attack and kill a person, typically by hanging, without involvement of the courts or legal system and often done by a mob

Manifesto: a written statement declaring publicly the intentions, motives, or views of its issuer

Manslaughter: the unlawful killing of a human being without express or implied intent

Martyrdom: the suffering of death on account of adherence to a cause and especially to one's religious faith

Mercenary: a man or woman who is paid by a foreign government or organization to fight in its service

Miscreant: one who behaves criminally or viciously

Molotov cocktail: an explosive weapon; each "cocktail" is a bottle filled with gasoline and wrapped in a rag or plugged with a wick, then ignited and thrown

Money laundering: to transfer illegally obtained money through an outside party to conceal the true source

Mule: a person who smuggles drugs inside his or her body

Mutinous: to resist lawful authority

Paramilitary: of, relating to, being, or characteristic of a force formed on a military pattern, especially as a potential auxiliary military force

Pathologist: a physician who specializes in examining tissue samples and fluids to diagnose diseases

PCR: polymerase chain reaction, a technique of making multiple copies of a small section of DNA so that it can be analyzed and identified

Personal alarm: a small electronic device that a person can carry and activate if he or she feels threatened

Phreaker: a person who hacks telephone systems

Pillory: a device formerly used for publicly punishing offenders consisting of a wooden frame with holes in which the head and hands can be locked

Political asylum: permitting foreigners to settle in your country to escape danger in another country, usually his or her native land

Postmortem: an autopsy; an examination of a dead body, looking for causes of death

Precedent: something done or said that serves as an example or rule to authorize or justify a subsequent act of similar kind

Pyramid scheme: an investment swindle in which some early investors are paid off with money put up by later ones in order to encourage more and bigger risks; also called a Ponzi scheme

Quick: the living flesh beneath the fingernails

Racketeering: the act of conducting a fraudulent scheme or activity

Ratchet: a mechanism consisting of a "pawl," a hinged catch that slips into sloping teeth of a cogwheel, so that it can be turned only in one direction

Repatriation: returning a person to his or her country of origin

Ruse: a subterfuge in order to distract someone's attention

Screw: slang term for a prison guard

Scuttle: to cut a hole through the bottom, deck, or side of a ship

Seditious: of, relating to, or tending toward an incitement of resistance to or insurrection against lawful authority

Serology: the laboratory analysis of blood serum, particularly in the detection of blood groups and antibodies

Siege (n.): a standoff situation, in which a group holds a position by force and refuses to surrender

Slander: a false and defamatory oral statement about a person

Smash and grab: a term used to describe a method of stealing, where thieves break windows (for example, on a shop front or a car) to grab the goods within before fleeing

Statute: a law enacted by the legislative branch of a government

Statutory: authorized by the statute that defines the law

Subversive: characterized by systematic attempts to overthrow or undermine a government or political system by persons working secretly from within

Succinylcholine: a synthetic drug that paralyzes muscle fiber

Vendetta: an often-prolonged series of retaliatory, vengeful, or hostile acts or exchange of such acts

White-collar crime: crime committed by office staff, usually involving theft from the company they work for

Worm: a computer program that enters one computer and replicates itself to spread to other computers; unlike a virus, it does not have to attach itself to other files

Xenophobic: having an unreasonable fear of what is foreign and especially of people of foreign origin

CHRONOLOGY

These are some of the main landmarks in the protection of civil rights in the United States:

1808: January 1, Congress passes a law forbidding the importation of slaves into the United States.

1841: March 9, Supreme Court rules on the *Amistad* case, upholding a lower-court decision to free the slaves so they can return to Africa.

1863: January 1, President Abraham Lincoln issues the Emancipation Proclamation, freeing slaves in the Confederate states.

1865: December 6, the 13th Amendment is ratified, abolishing slavery in all states.

1866: July 10, Congress overturns President Andrew Johnson's veto of its act to help the Freedmen's Bureau protect the rights of freed slaves.

1868: July 14, the 14th Amendment is ratified, giving citizenship to former slaves.

1870: February 8, the 15th Amendment is ratified, assuring the vote for all races.

1875: March 1, Congress passes a law giving equal rights to blacks in public accommodations and on jury duty (but the U.S. Supreme Court abolishes this act in 1883).

1944: April 3, Supreme Court rules that a person cannot be denied a vote in the Democratic primary election in Texas because of his or her color.

1946: June 3, the U.S. Supreme Court rules that any seat on interstate buses must be available to all races.

1948: July 26, President Harry S. Truman issues an executive order banning segregation in the U.S. armed forces and in federal employment.

1950: June 5, Supreme Court upholds blacks' right to attend state law schools and receive full benefits from the schools.

1954: May 17, the U.S. Supreme Court rules against segregation in education.

1957: April 29, Congress passes the first civil rights legislation in the 20th century to protect voting rights.

1964: July 2, President Lyndon B. Johnson signs a general civil rights act that bars discrimination in voting, employment, and public accommodations.

1965: August 6, Congress passes the Voting Rights Act, creating federal registrars to ensure that state officials cannot refuse to register black voters.

1968: Martin Luther King, Jr. assassinated.

1971: Schools start using busing to desegregate public schools.

1983: President Ronald Reagan designates January 15 "Martin Luther King, Jr. Day."

1991: President George Bush signs Civil Rights Act of 1991.

1992: Rodney King riots in Los Angeles.

2005: Edgar Ray Killen, leader of 1964 Mississippi civil rights murders, convicted of manslaughter 41 years after the crimes.

2009: U.S. Supreme Court in *Ricci v. DeStefano* found that white firefighters had been victims of reverse discrimination.

2013: U.S. Supreme Court strikes down certain portions of the Voting Rights Act.

2014: Riots in Ferguson, Missouri, after a white police officer shot and killed a black man, Michael Brown.

FURTHER INFORMATION

Useful Web Sites

Anti-Defamation League: www.adl.org

British National Party: www.bnp.org.uk

Bureau of Justice Statistics: http://www.bjs.gov

Institute of Race Relations: www.irr.org.uk

Southern Poverty Law Center: www.splcenter.org

The Nobel Biography of Martin Luther King, Jr.: www.nobel.se/peace/laureates/1964/king-bio.html

U.S. Census Bureau: www.census.gov

Further Reading

Carnes, Jim. *Us and Them: A History of Intolerance in America*. New York: Oxford University Press, 1999.

Chakraborti, Neil. *Hate Crime: Impact, Causes, and Responses.* SAGE Publications, 2015.

Citron, Danielle. *Hate Crimes in Cyberspace.* Cambridge, MA: Harvard University Press, 2014.

Espero, Roman. *What Is a Hate Crime?* San Diego: Greenhaven Press, 2001.

Freemon, David K. *The Jim Crow Laws and Racism in American History*. Springfield, New Jersey: Enslow Publishers, 2000.

Gerstenfeld, Phyllis. *Hate Crimes: Causes, Controls, and Controversies.* SAGE Publications, 2001.

Hoskins, James. *Separate But Not Equal: The Dream and the Struggle*. New York: Scholastic, Inc., 2002.

Levine, Ellen. *Freedom's Children: Young Civil Rights Activists Tell Their Own Stories*. New York: Puffin, 2000.

Levine, Ellen. *If You Lived at the Time of Martin Luther King*. New York: Scholastic, Inc. 1994.

Steffoff, Rebecca. *Nelson Mandela: A Hero for Democracy*. New York: Fawcett Books, 1994.

Webster-Doyle, Terence. *Why Is Everybody Always Picking on Us?: Understanding the Roots of Prejudice*. New York: Weatherhill, Inc., 2000.

Williams, Kidaba. *They Left Great Marks on Me: African American Testimonies of Racial Violence from Emancipation to World War I*. New York: NYU Press, 2012.

About the Author

Dr. John D. Wright is an American writer and editor living in England. He has been a reporter for *Time* and *People* magazines in their London bureaus, covering such subjects as politics, crime, and social welfare. He has also been a journalist for the U.S. Navy and for newspapers in Alabama and Tennessee. He holds a Ph.D. degree in Communications from the University of Texas, taught journalism at three Southern universities, and was chairman of the Department of Mass Communications at Emory & Henry College in Virginia. He has published a dictionary, *The Language of the Civil War*, and an encyclopedia of space exploration. He has contributed to many reference books, including the Oxford University Press *New Dictionary of National Biography* (under production), Reader's Digest *Facts at Your Fingertips* (2001), and the *Oxford Guide to British and American Culture* (1999).

INDEX

Adams, John Quincy 12
African National Congress (ANC) 57, 60, 64–65, 67, 69
Afrikaner National Party 58
Albanians 16–17
Ali, Muhammad (Cassius Clay) 36
Amistad rebellion 12–13
Anti-Defamation League 42, 93
anti-Semitism 25, 42, 78, 83
apartheid 57–60, 62–69, 74, 84
Arabs 10, 12, 21, 42, 74, 78, 84
Asians 10, 41, 58–59, 73, 79, 80, 83–84
Austria 18, 76–78

Baldwin, Roger Sherman 12
Bantus 57–59
barbarian 11
Biko, Steve 62, 69–70
black or African Americans 10, 25, 30–32, 34–36, 38–41, 48
  oppression 30
  riots by 39–41, 51
Black Church Group 55
Black Consciousness Movement 69
Black Panther Party 35
Bosnia 16, 83
Botha, P.W. 65
Britain 11, 58, 73, 79–80, 83
  minorities in 79–80
British National Party (BNP) 73, 83, 93
Broca, Pierre Paul 10–11
Burundi 20
Bush, George 65, 92
Bush, George W. 18
Byrd, James 41, 43

Canada 14, 21
Carlos, John 31
Carmichael, Stokely 50–51
Center for Democratic Renewal 42
civil rights 33–34, 37–43, 45–47, 50–51, 53, 62, 91–93
civil rights activist 37–39

Civil Rights Acts 34, 40, 43, 50, 92
coloreds 58
Conyers, John, Jr. 39
Cry Freedom 69

Davis, Jefferson 12
de Klerk, F.W. 65, 67–68
detention camps 34

Eisenhower, Dwight D. 40
ethnic cleansing 9, 15–16, 74
Europe 9, 11–12, 15–16, 18, 26, 28, 58–59, 73–74, 76, 78–79, 83–84
Evers, Medgar 37

Federal Bureau of Investigation (FBI) 41–43, 54
foreigners 9, 11, 30, 73–74, 82–83, 89
Fortuyn, Pim 78
France 9, 14, 16, 18, 74–75, 78, 84
freedom riders 34–35
Furrow, Buford, Jr. 41

Gandhi, Mahatma 47, 61
Germany 9, 15–16, 18, 54, 77–78
Grant, General Ulysses S. 30
guest workers 9, 18
gypsies 15, 84

Haider, Jorg 76
Hitler, Adolf 15
Holocaust 9, 15–16, 21, 74
homelands 26, 57, 59, 65
homosexuals 15
Hutus 20

immigration 16, 74, 76, 78, 83
  illegal 18, 74
Indonesia 84
integration 34–35, 37–38
intimidation 42, 82
Islam 18, 36, 41, 78
Israelis 14, 21

Japanese Americans 34
Jews 9, 15–16, 25, 30, 74, 78, 83

Johnson, Lyndon B. 40, 50–51, 92

Kennedy, John F. 26, 40
Kennedy, Robert 51
King, Coretta Scott 46–47, 49
King, Dexter 53
King, Martin Luther, Jr. 34, 37, 39, 45–55, 61, 64, 92–93
King, Martin Luther III 46
King, Rodney 40–41, 92
Kosovo 16, 83
Kruser, Gary 57
Ku Klux Klan 25, 29–30, 43

Lawrence, Stephen 80–81
Le Pen, Jean-Marie 74–75
Linnaeus, Carolus 10
lynchings 32, 74

Malcolm X 35–37, 50
Mandela, Nelson 60, 62, 64–69, 94
Mississippi Burning (MIBURN) 43
Mugabe, Robert 84–85
Muhammad, Elijah 36

Nation of Islam 36
National Association for the Advancement of Colored People (NAACP) 37, 39
nationalism 9, 14–15
Native Americans 10, 26, 28
Nazis 9, 15–16
neo-Nazis 78, 82–84

Olympic Games 31
Organization of Afro-American Unity 36–37

Palestinians 14, 21
Parks, Rosa 39–40, 46
passive resistance 61
political asylum 9, 16, 89

race 9–12, 14–15, 26, 30–32, 34, 37–38, 41–43, 49, 51, 57–59, 67–68, 73, 78, 80–82, 84
  classification in South Africa 57–59

classification in U.S. 10–11
concept of 9–21
race crimes, statistics 41–43
racial hatred, inciting 30, 43
racism, fight against 42–43
Ray, James Earl 53–54
Reagan, Ronald 45, 92
Reeb, James 37
Reno, Janet 53
Russia 78, 82–83
Rwanda 20, 84

sanctions 57, 65, 76
schools, segregation 34, 40, 59, 91
segregation 30, 33–35, 37, 39–40, 45–46, 49, 57–58, 68, 91
Serbia/Serbs 16–17, 83
Sharpeville massacre 60
skinheads 73, 83
slave laborers 12, 76
slavery 9, 12, 30, 74, 84, 91
Smith, Tommie 31
South Africa 57–62, 64–69, 74, 84
Southern Poverty Law Center 42, 93
Soweto 62, 66
Spain 83–84

Trail of Tears 26
Truman, Harry S. 33–34, 91
Truth and Reconciliation Commission 57, 63, 67, 69
Tutsis 20
Tutu, Desmond 62, 65–66, 74

United Nations 21, 62, 65

Van Buren, Martin 12

Wallace, George 37–38
World War II 9, 15–16, 34, 78–79, 82

Index 95

PICTURE CREDITS

Front Cover: Robin Nelson/ZUMA Press/Newscom: Klu Klux Klan rally and cross burning in Virginia

Picture Credits: 8, duncan1890/iStock; 11, The British Library; 13, Picture History/Newscom; 14, Everett Historical/Shutterstock; 15, Topham Picturepoint; 17, Topham Picturepoint; 19, Joel Carillet/iStock; 20, Topham Picturepoint; 22, Topham Picturepoint; 24, Topham Picturepoint; 27, Topham Picturepoint; 28, Tami Freed/Shutterstock; 29, Topham Picturepoint; 31, Topham Picturepoint; 32, Popperfoto; 33, Topham Picturepoint; 35, Topham Picturepoint; 36, Topham Picturepoint; 37, Topham Picturepoint; 38, Topham Picturepoint; 39, Topham Picturepoint; 40, Topham Picturepoint; 42, ginosphotos/iStock; 44, Topham Picturepoint; 46, Topham Picturepoint; 47, Topham Picturepoint; 48, Topham Picturepoint; 50, Topham Picturepoint; 51, Topham Picturepoint; 52, Chine Nouvelle/SIPA/Newscom; 54, Everett Collection/Newscom; 55, Topham Picturepoint; 56, Topham Picturepoint; 58, Topham Picturepoint; 59, Topham Picturepoint; 60, Popperfoto; 61, Topham Picturepoint; 62, Topham Picturepoint; 63, Topham Picturepoint; 64, Popperfoto; 66, Topham Picturepoint; 67, Topham Picturepoint; 68, Topham Picturepoint; 70, REX/Newscom; 72, Topham Picturepoint; 74, Popperfoto; 75, Enrico Dagnino/Black Star/Newscom; 76, Popperfoto; 77, Popperfoto; 79, Topham Picturepoint; 81, Topham Picturepoint; 83, Popperfoto; 85, Popperfoto